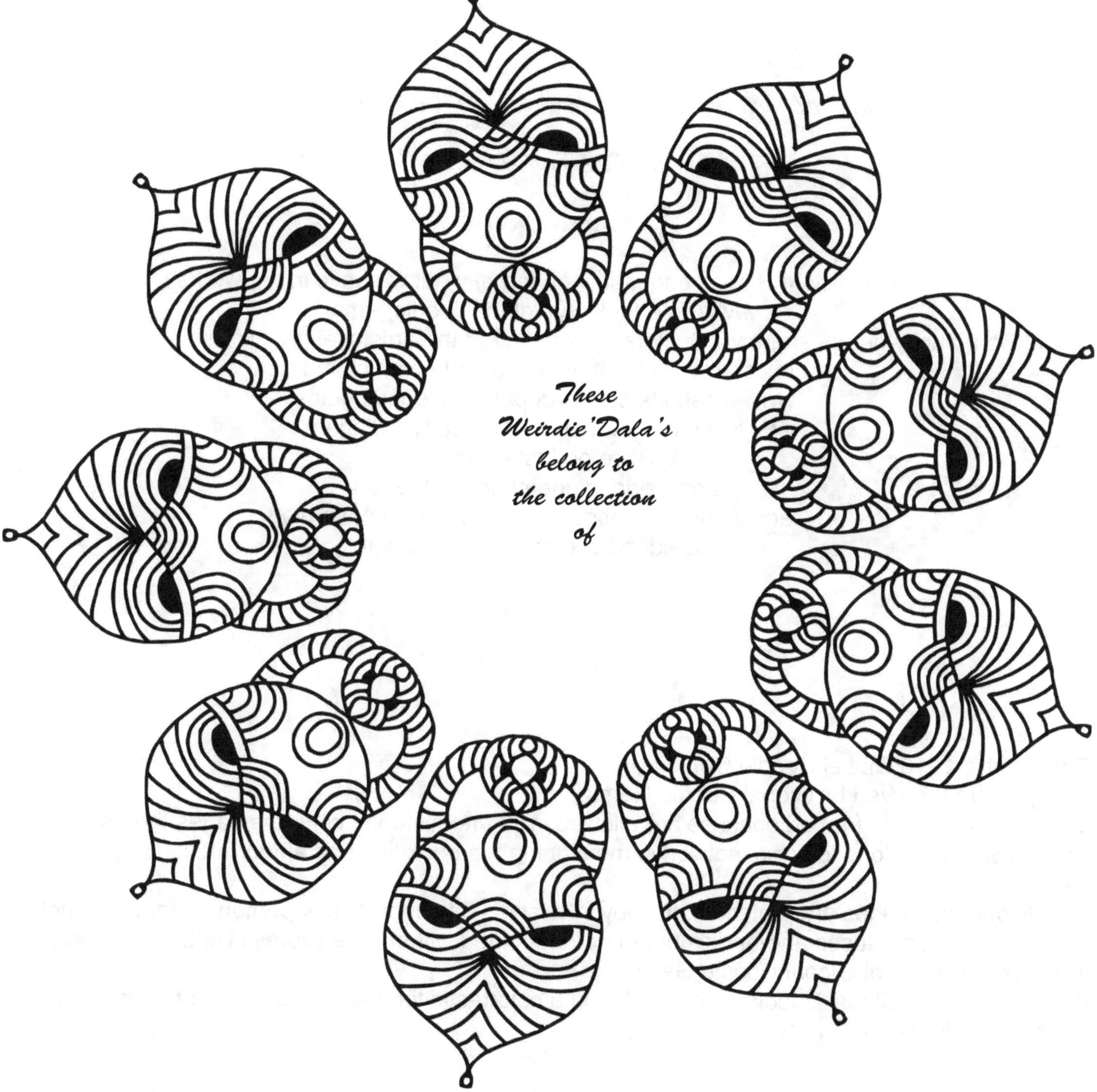

These Weirdie 'Dala's belong to the collection of

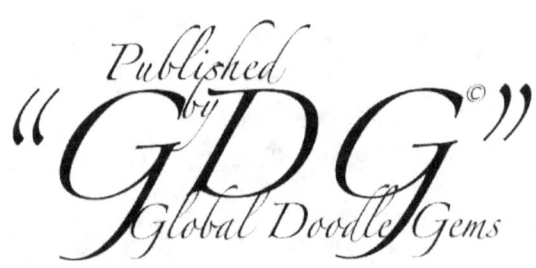

Share your colored versions with us ! We love seeing your results and hearing from you we are social !

The Official FB book page, stay on top of what we have in the works !
www.facebook.com/globaldoodlegems
The Community group, share your colored pages, meet the artists, enjoy exclusive freebies, take part in community Charity books and so much more......
www.facebook.com/groups/globaldoodlegems/
Follow us on Twitter.... @GlobalDoodlegem
We are on Instagram too
@globaldoodlegems for instagram
...and if you are not social like that we have a blog
globaldoodlegems.wordpress.com

Copyright © 2016 Global Doodle Gems
All rights are reserved by Global Doodle Gems.
Duplication of pages for personal use are allowed. You are invited to color the pages then scan/post your coloured versions to social networks, mentioning the book title and author/artist (Global Doodle Gems).
All artwork and images are protected by copyright laws. This book or any portion thereof may not, otherwise, be reproduced and/or distributed or transmitted without the express written permission of the artist/publisher of Global Doodle Gems.
All of us from the Global Doodle Gems wish you a colortastic time and look forward to seeing your wonderful color results online !

Welcome to my world of Weirdies

This series of drawings are dedicated to all the weird, whimsical,
wacky and totally amazing people in the world !
Through art and coloring I have met and befriended
so many amazing personalities,
and come to discover just how awesome,
incredible and giving strangers can be,
and how fast a stranger can become a dearly loved
friend, through the coloring world I have met
amazing artists and stunning colorists,
I have been overwhelmed and delighted by this
amazing journey of discovery and
discovering new corners of my imagination and art,
the 'Weirdie'Dala's is an opening book
to a dedication of a Weirdie a day series !
I will make 12 books, one for each month of the year, with
a Weirdie for each day.... some of the Weirdies can also
be colored upside down... in the books I will include
upside down extras of those Weirdies that may apply...
The first of the 12 books will be out soon...
follow me on my artpage facebook AMVART
I will try to post my colored daily ...
and keep you updated on new releases.
Please feel free to share yours with me ...
I would love to see them...
I hope you will enjoy my Weirdie World
Starting with 50 Weirdie'Dala's.
Sending out a huge embrace to all of you !

Maria Wedel

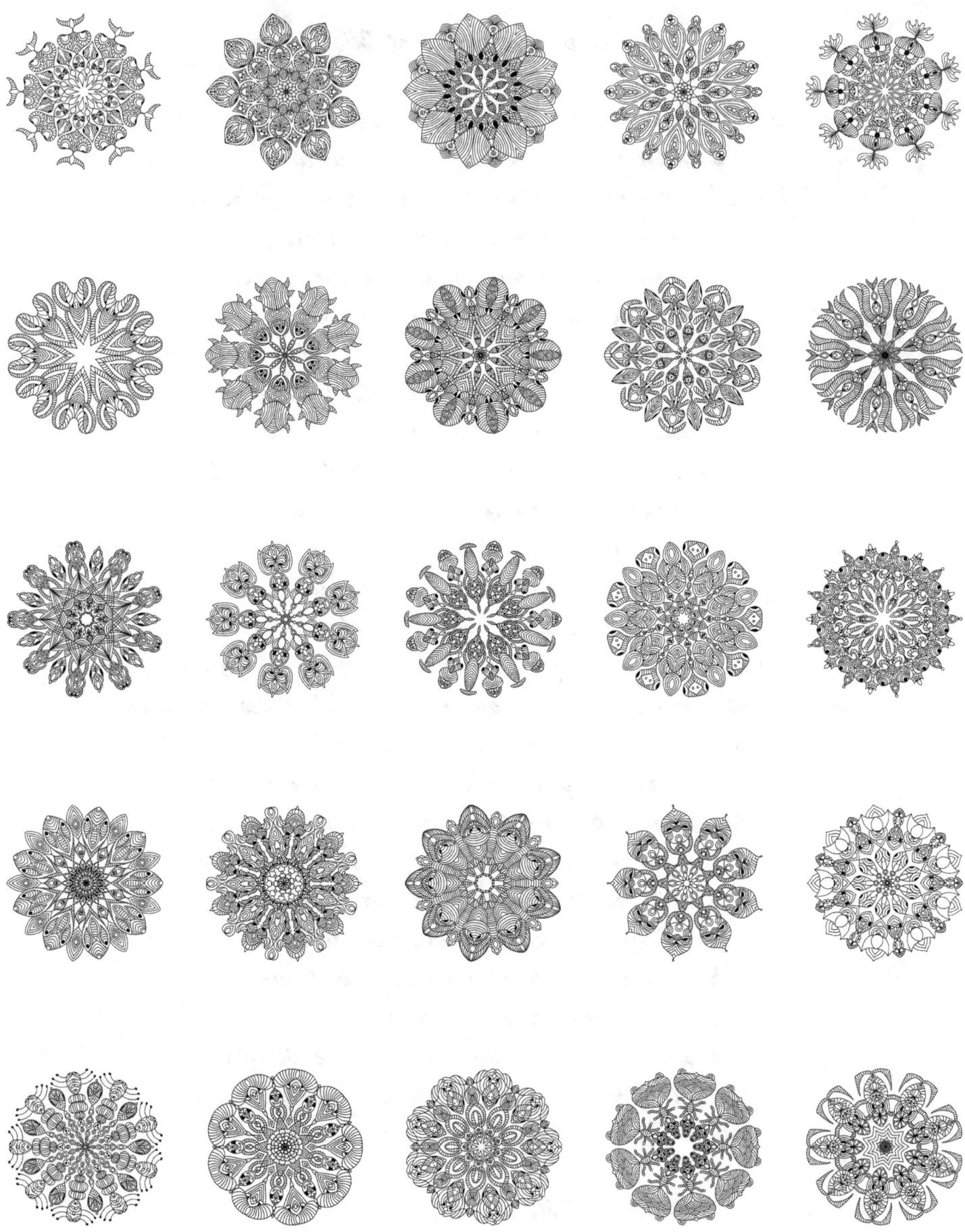

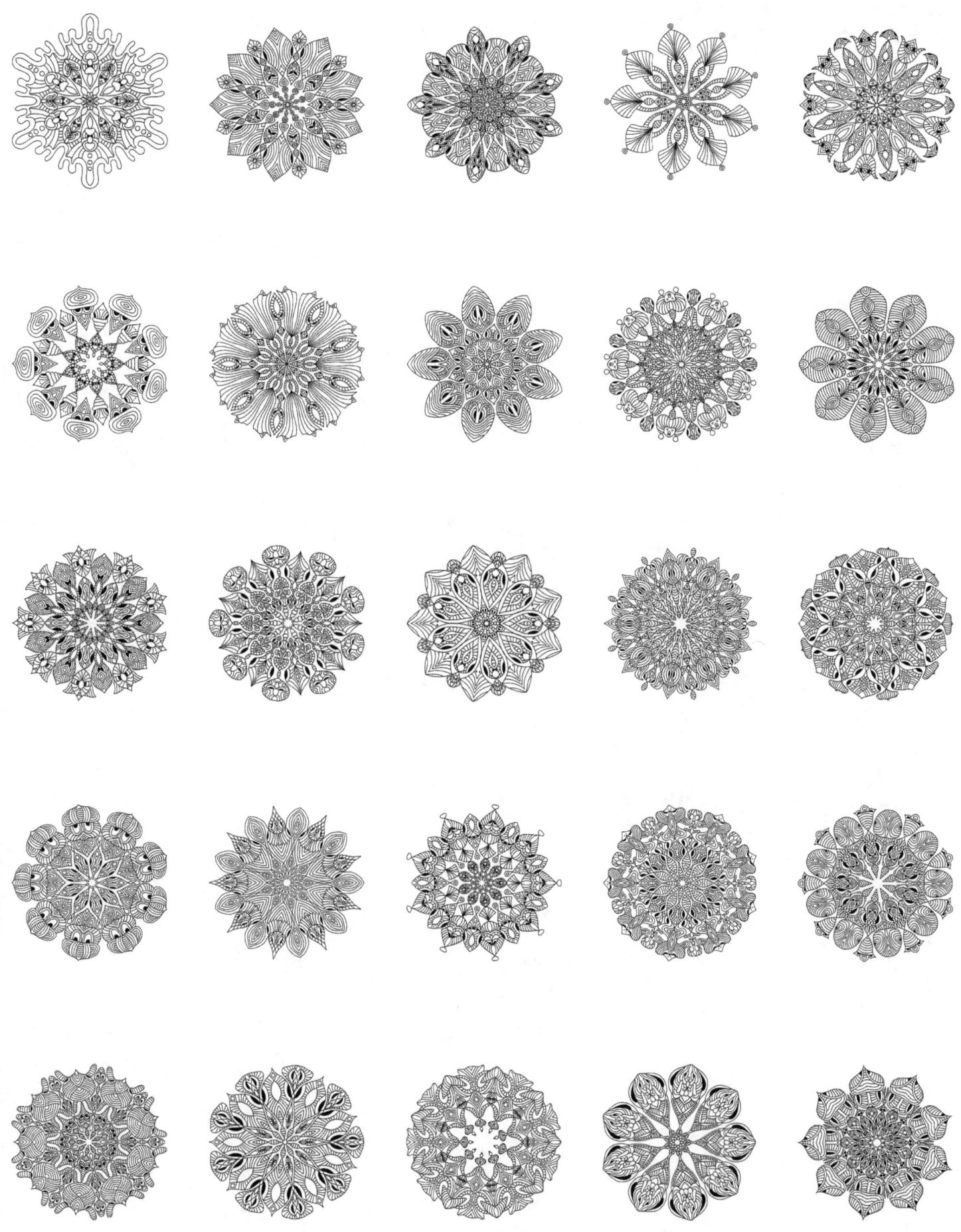

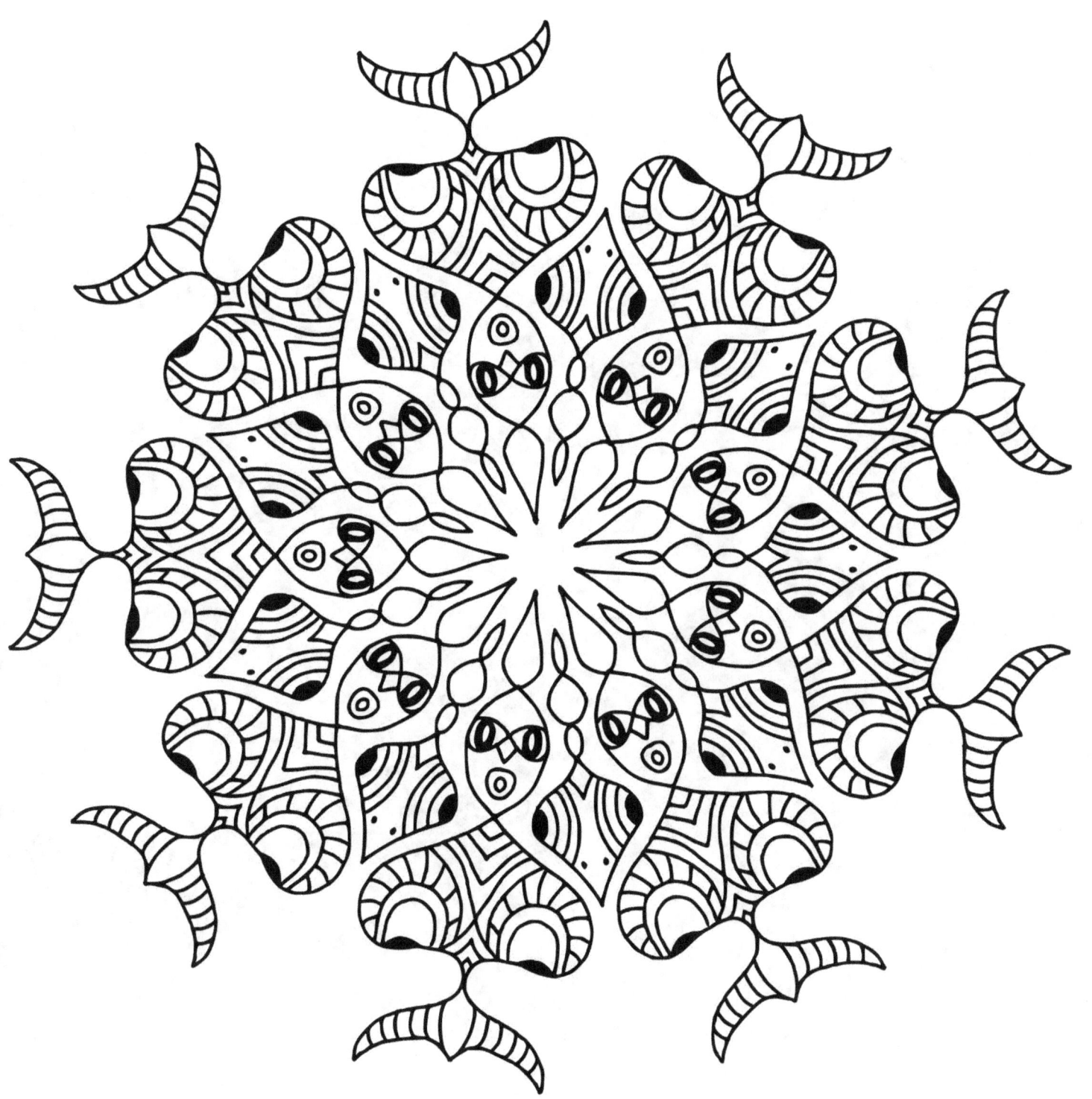

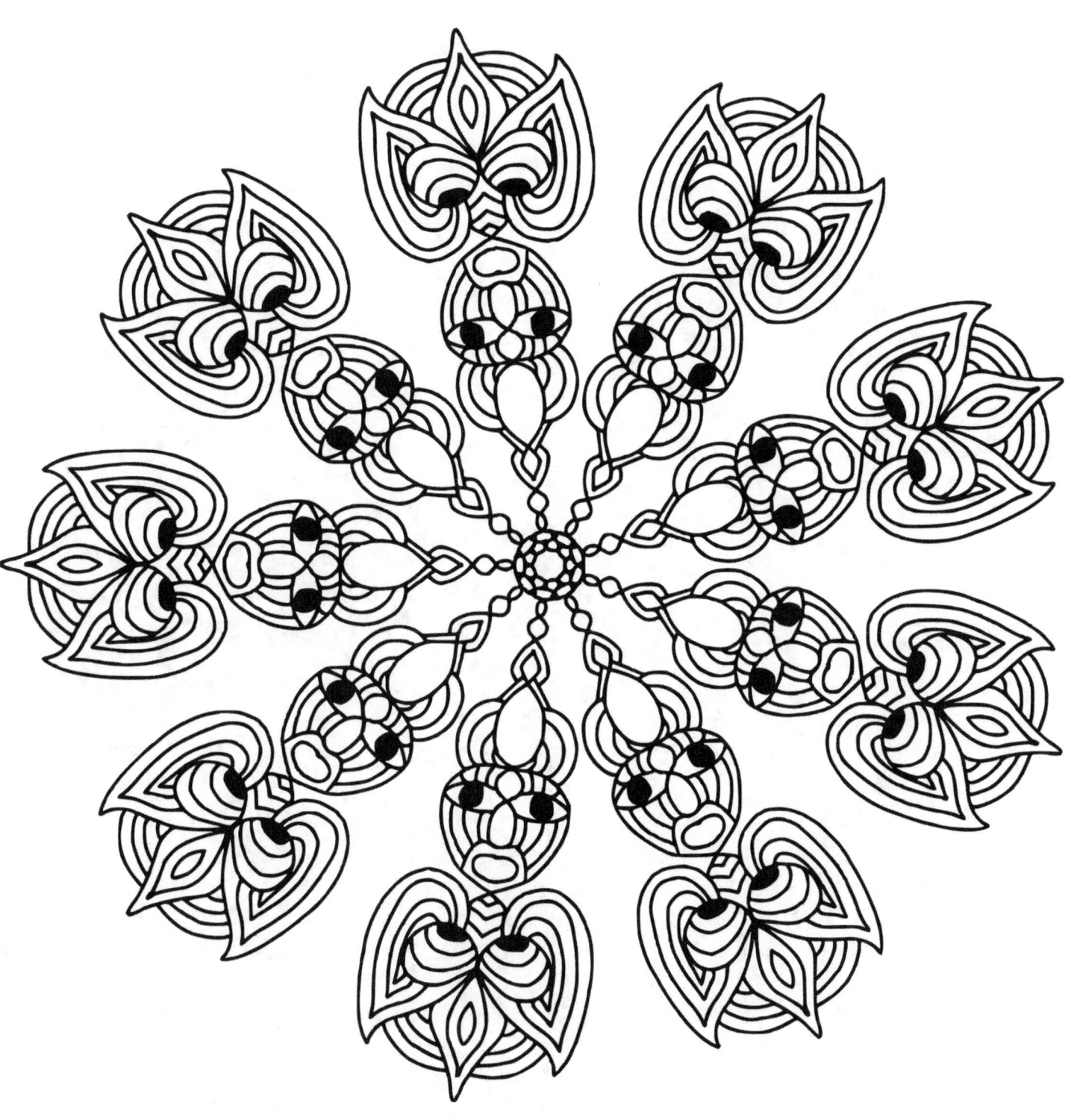

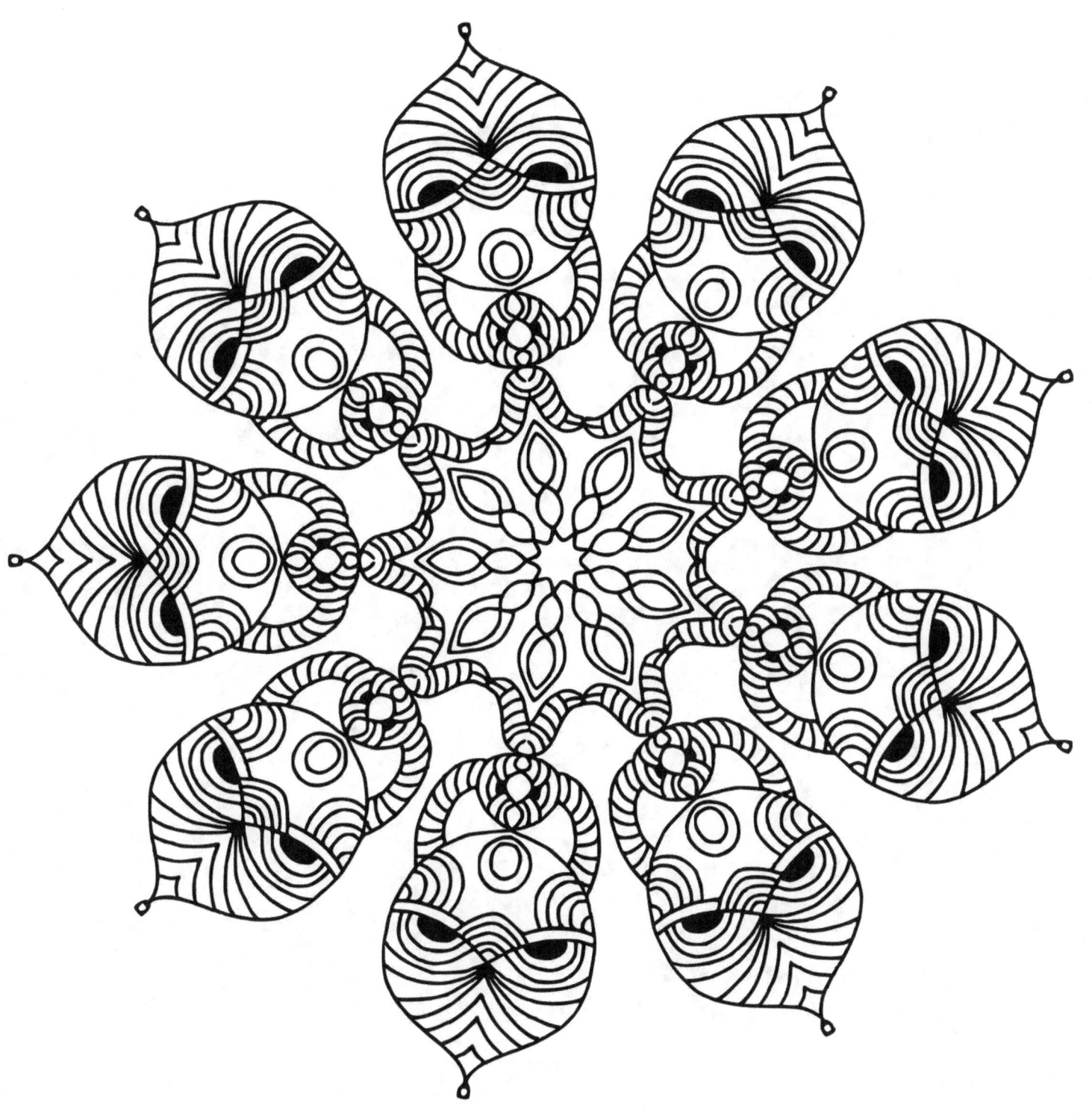

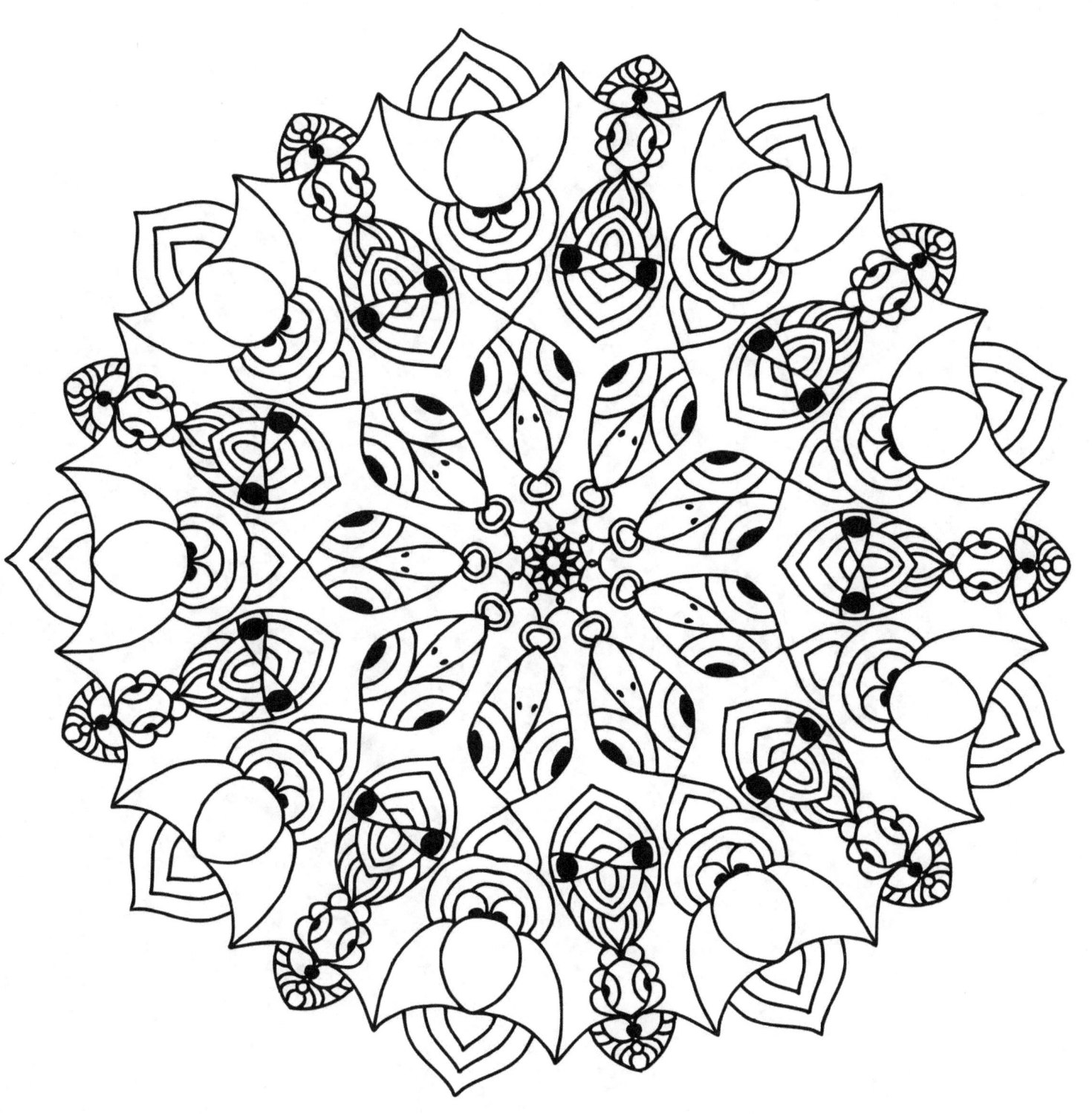

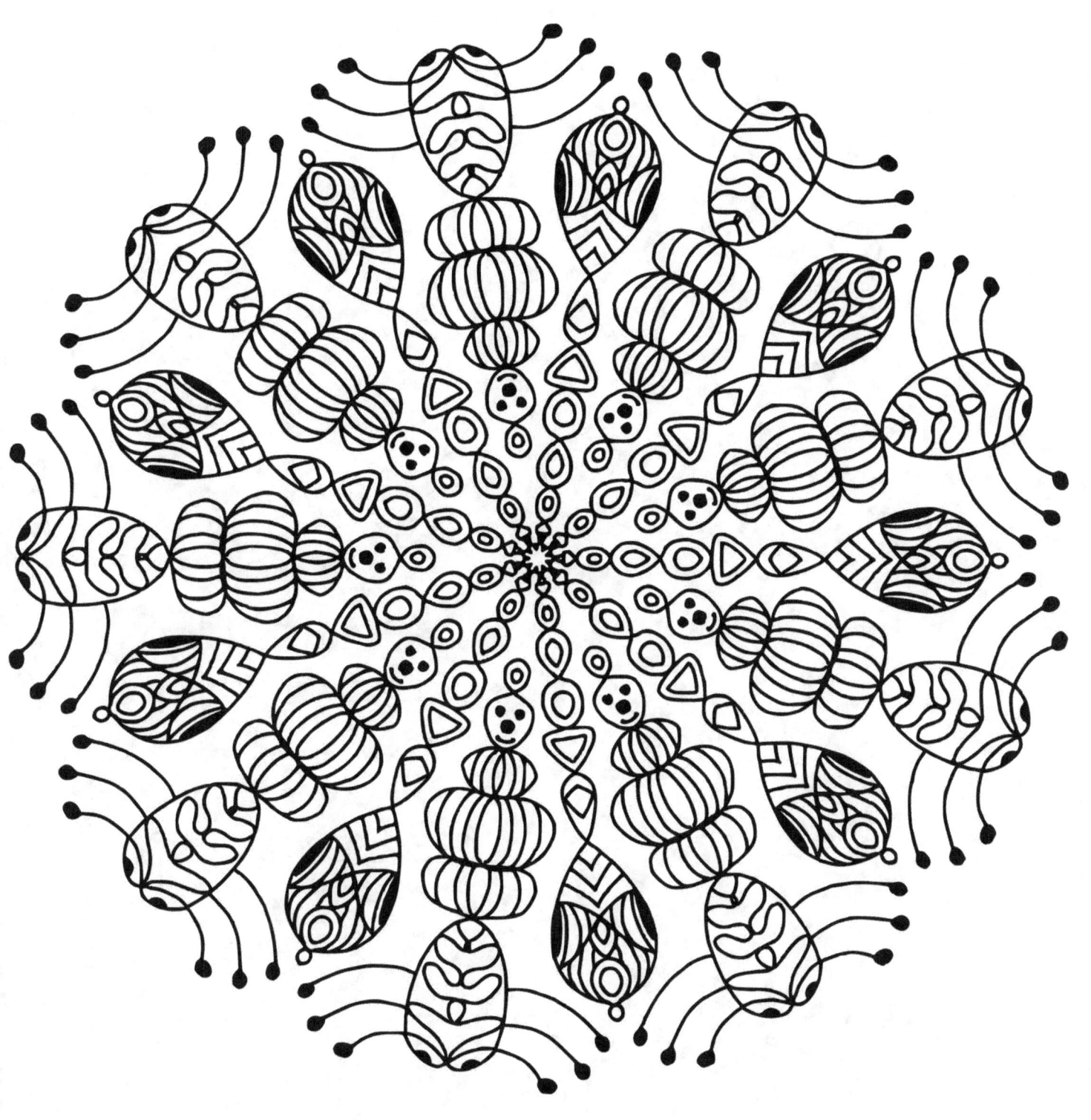

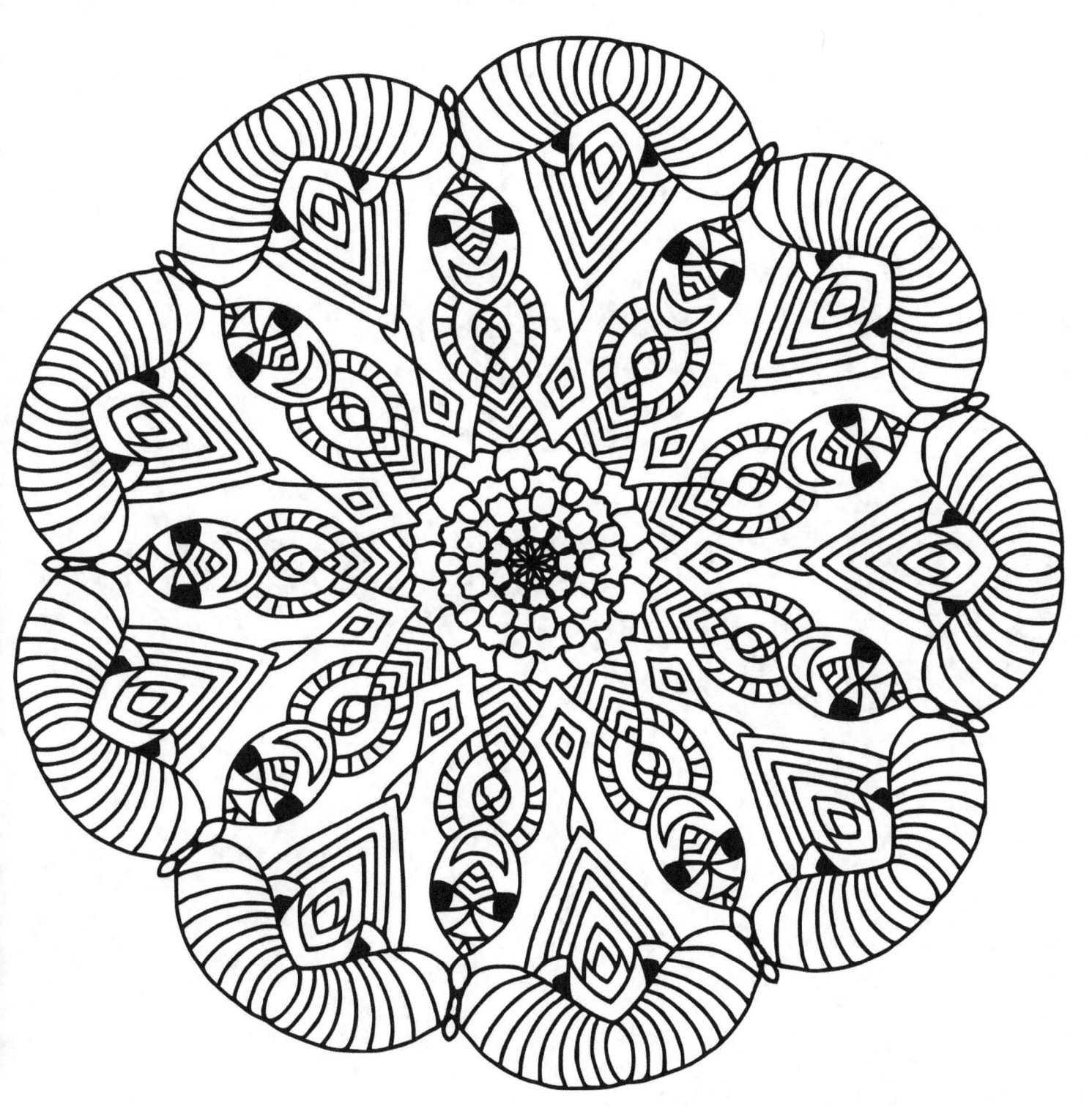

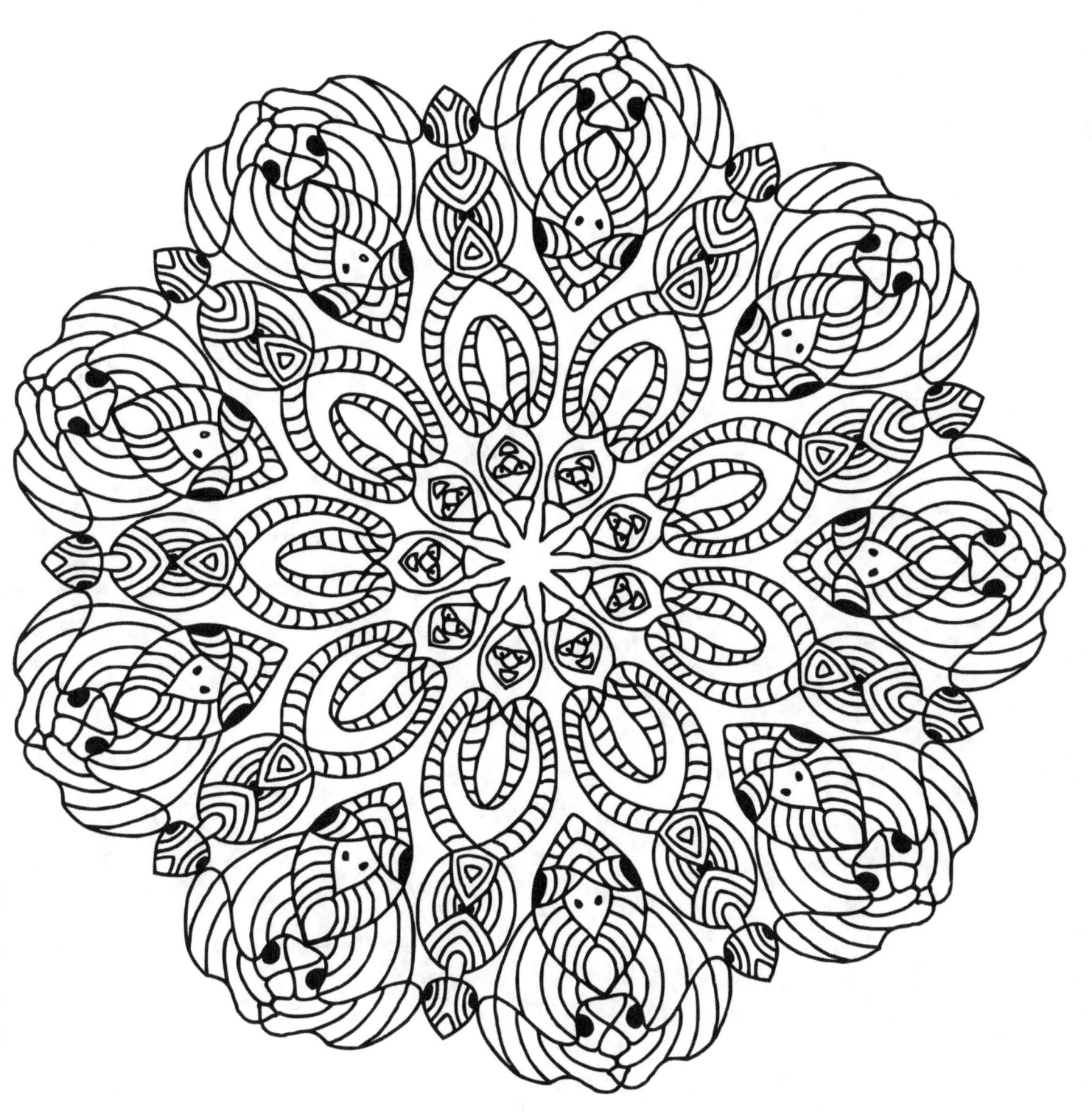

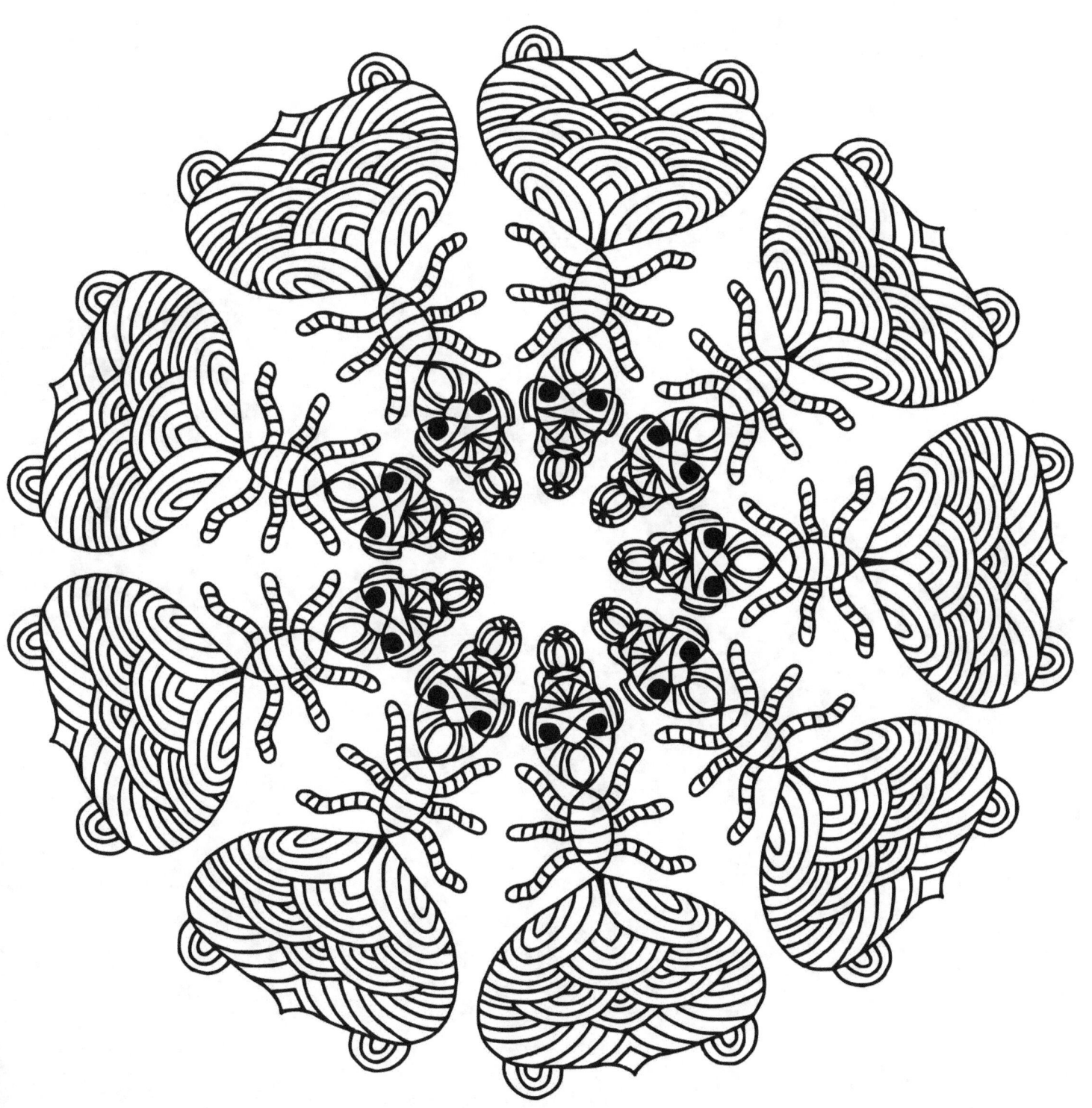

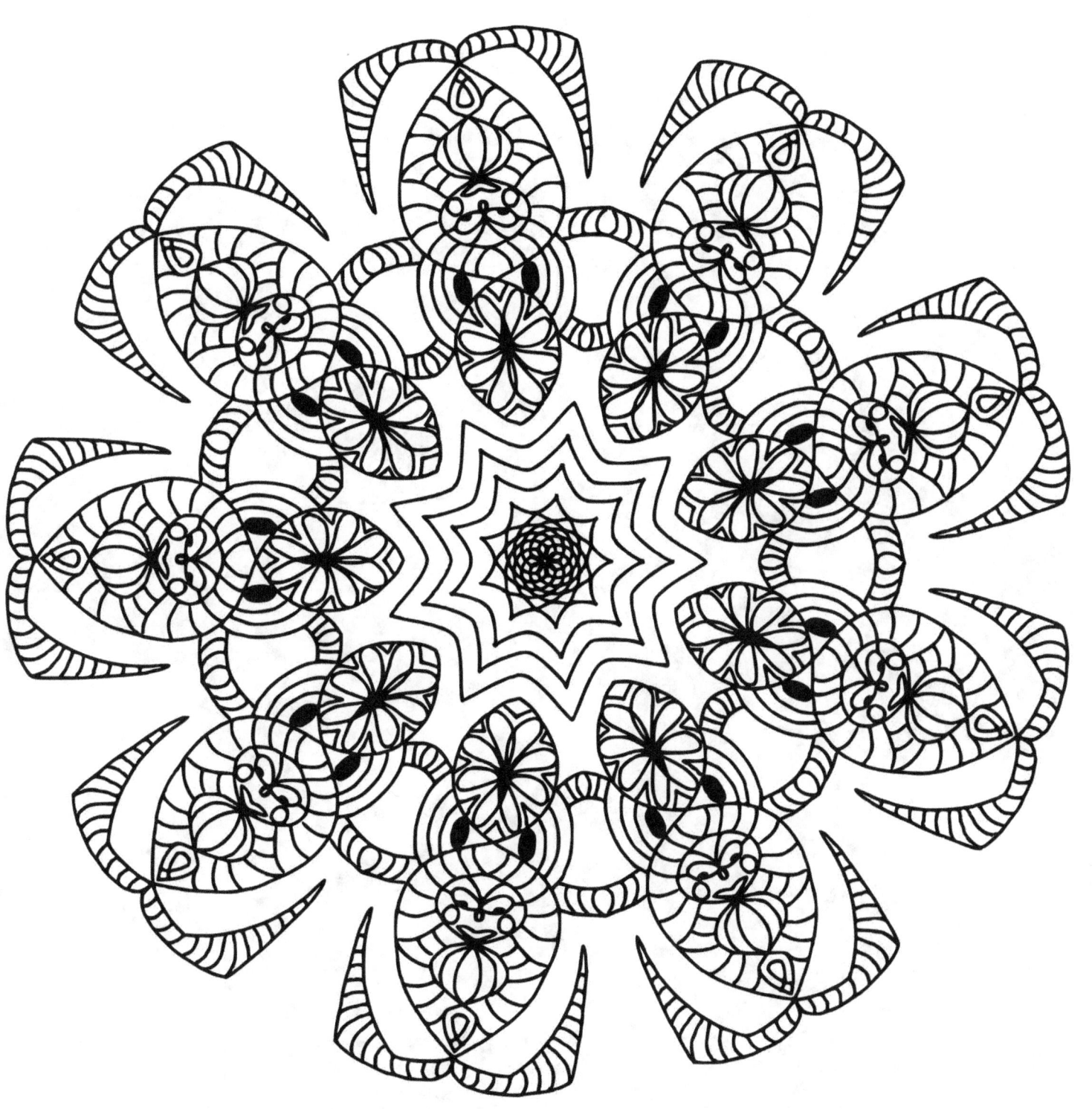

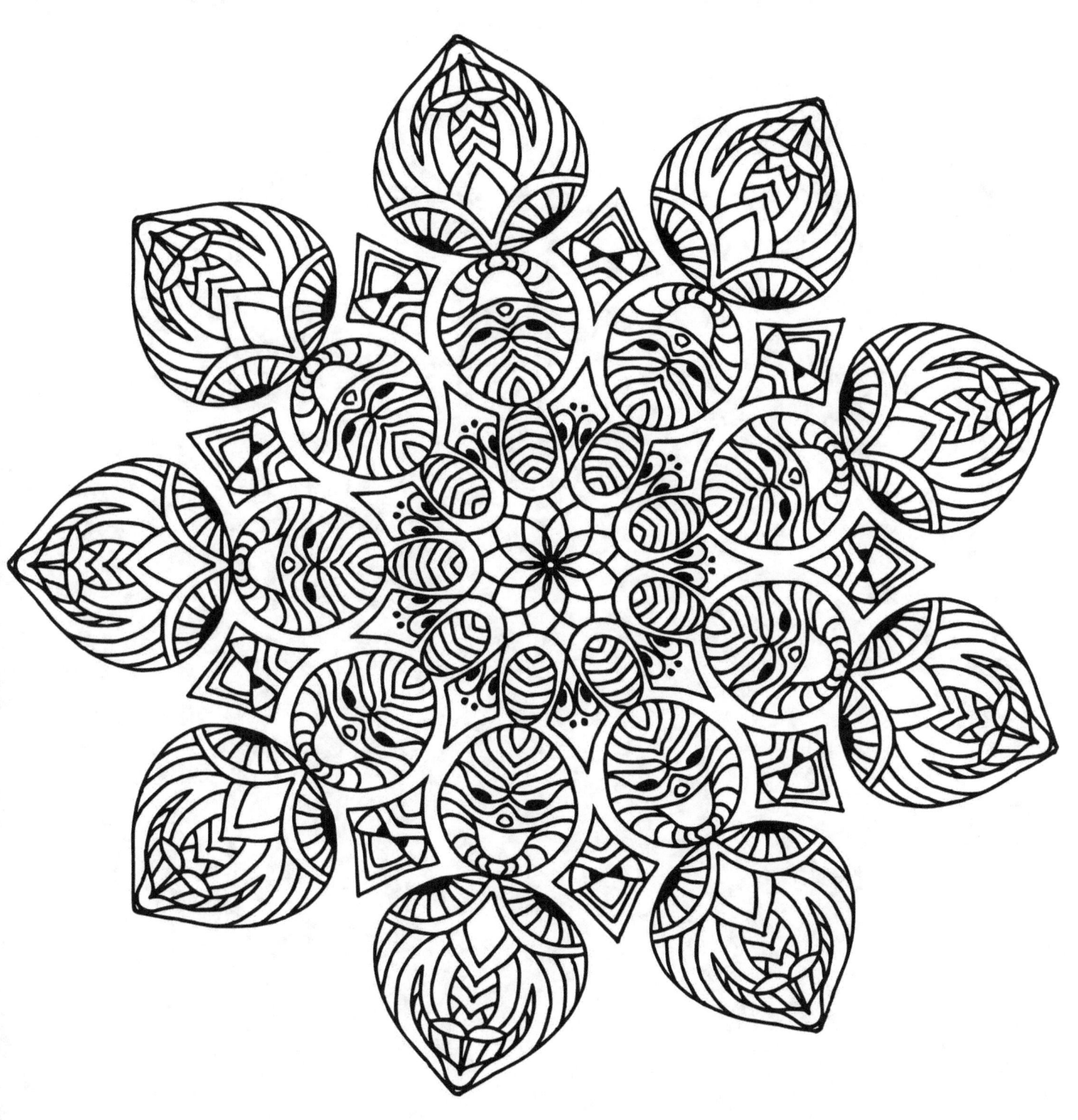

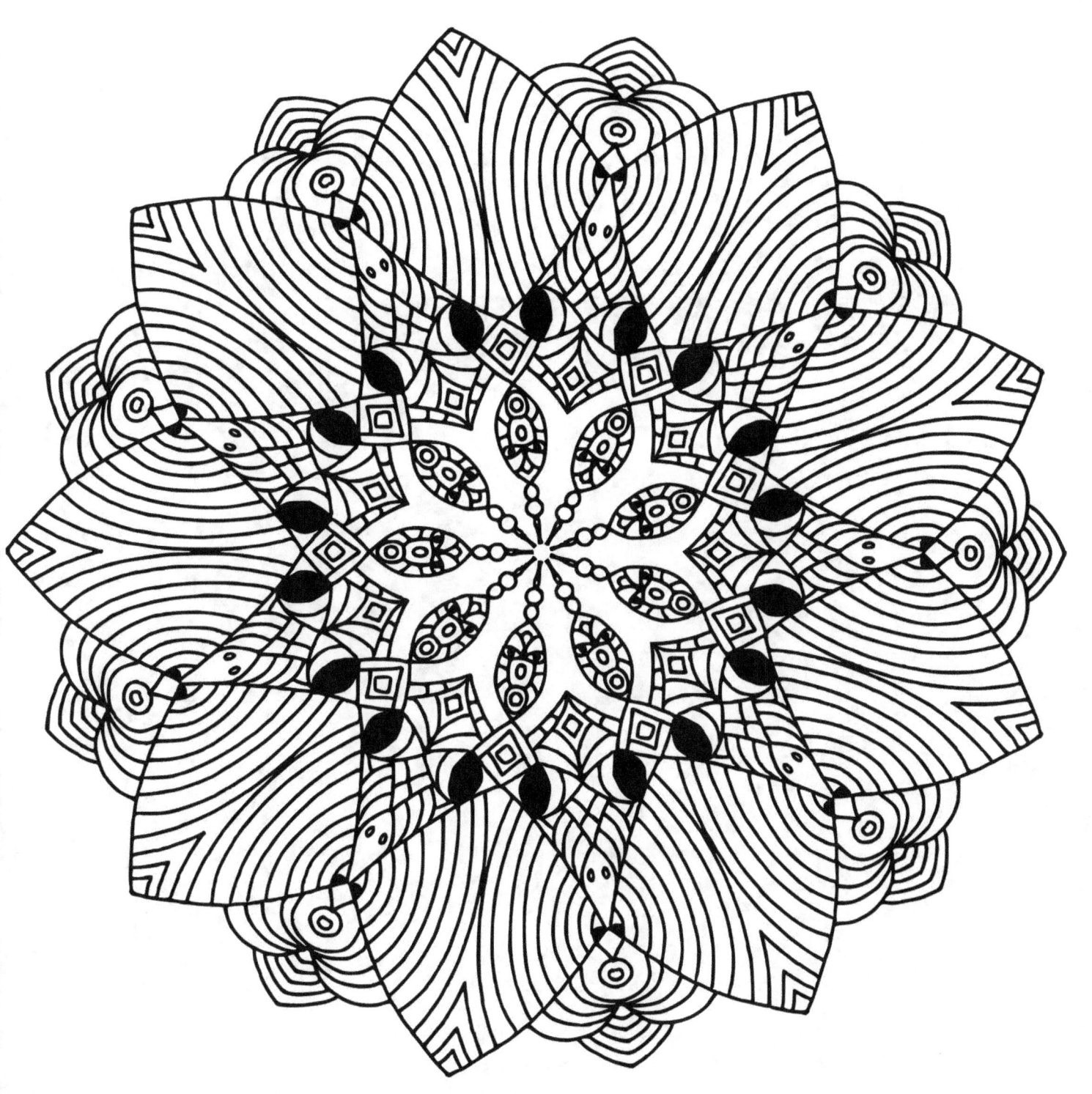

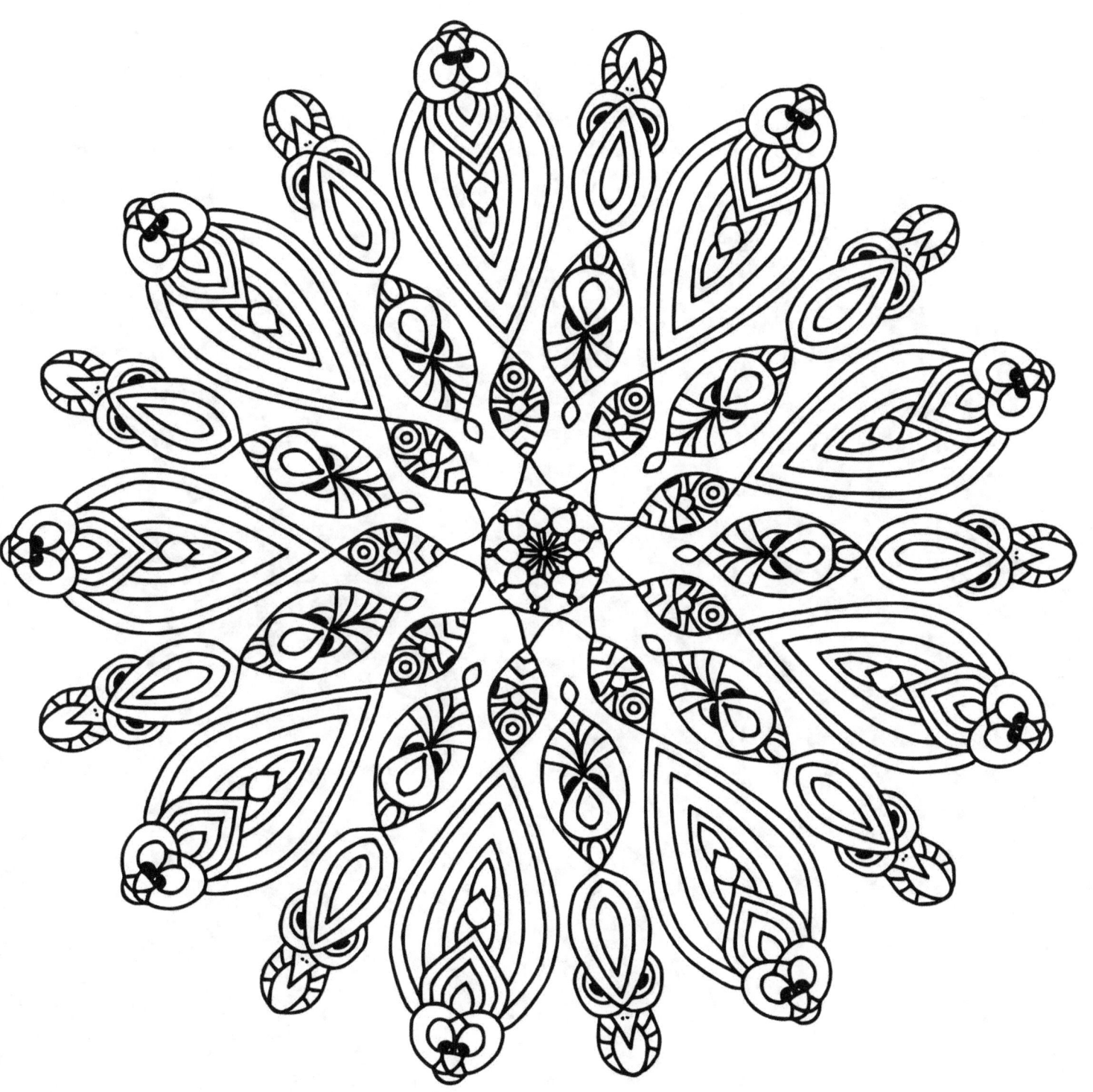

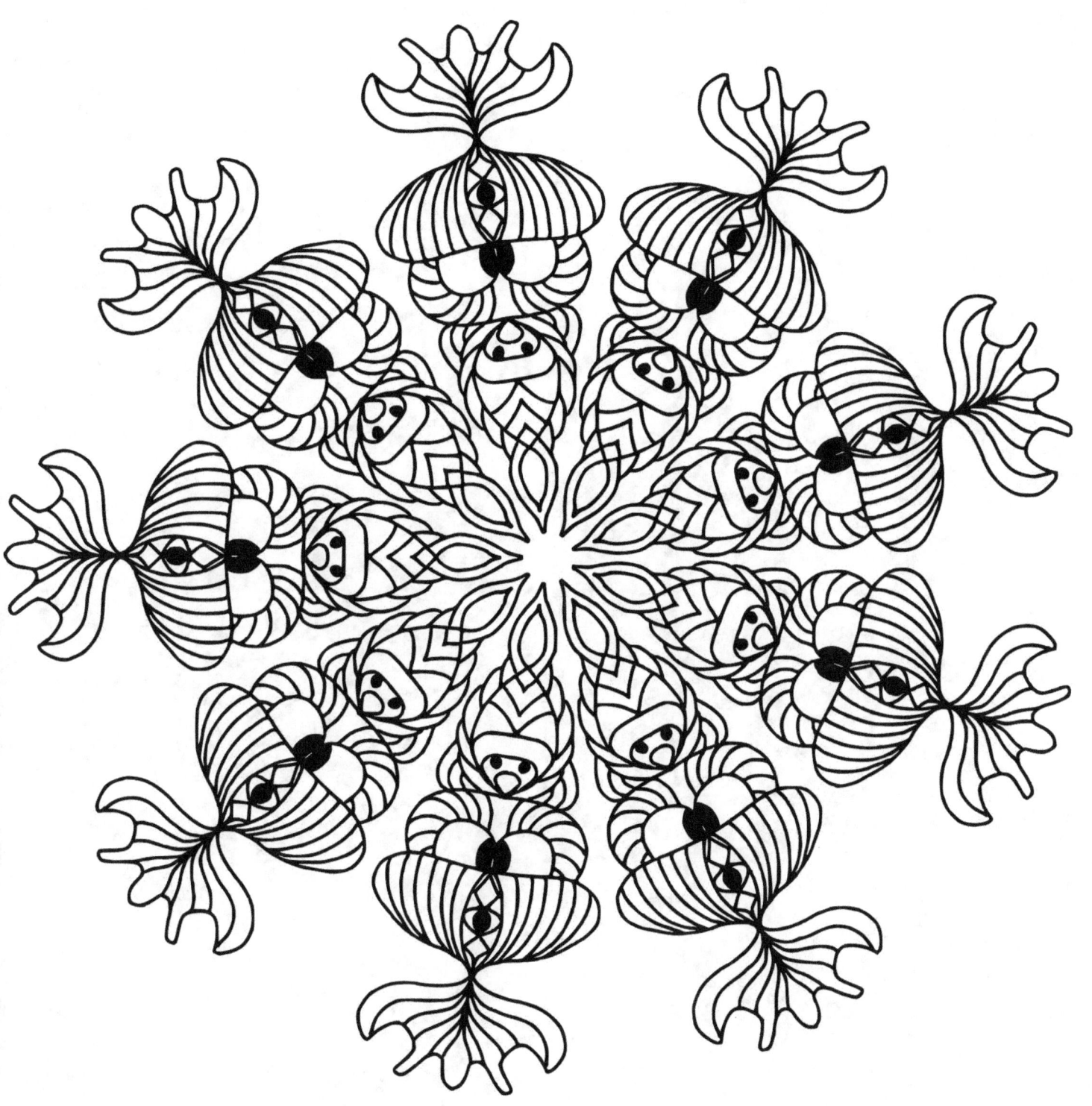

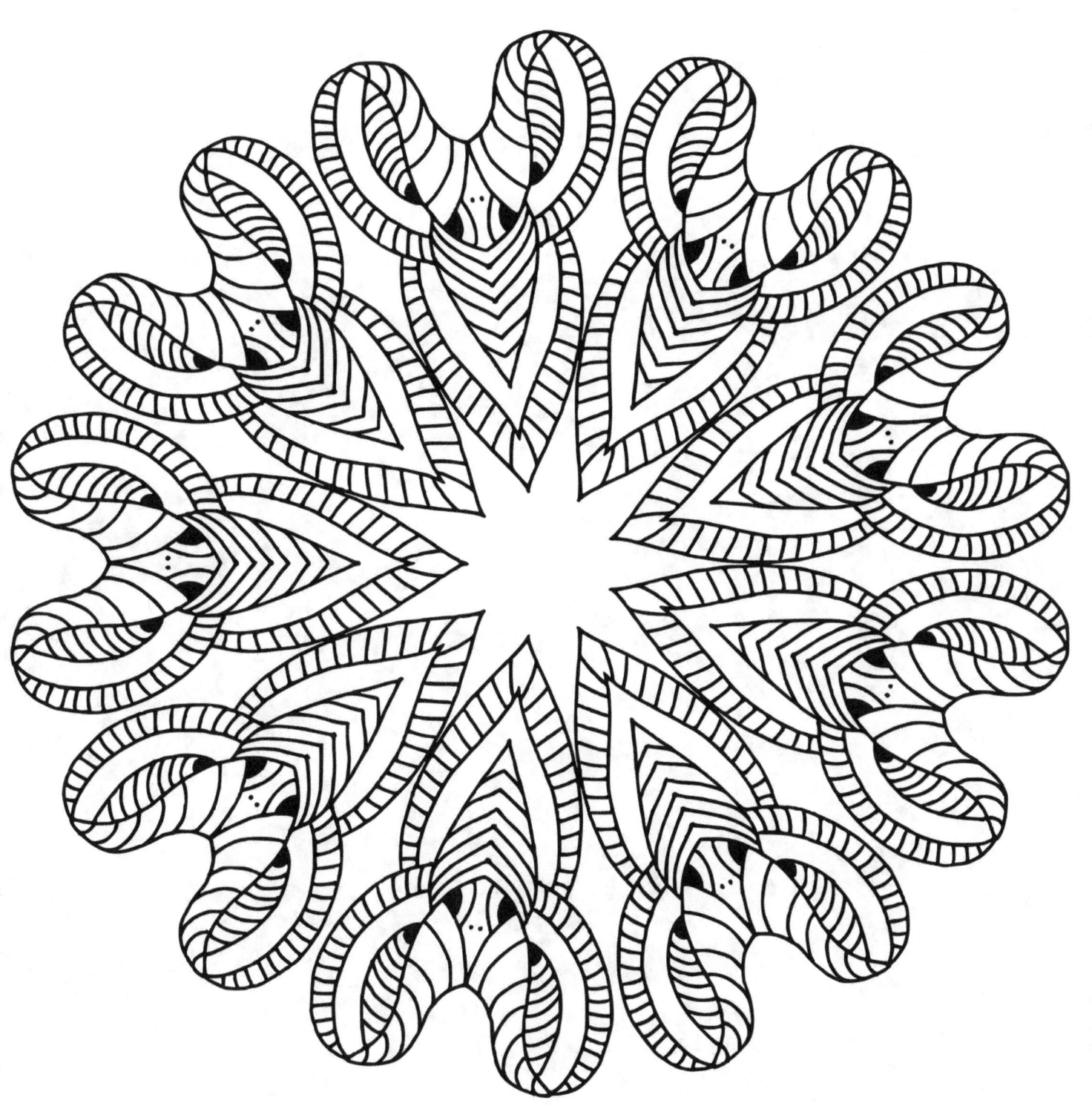

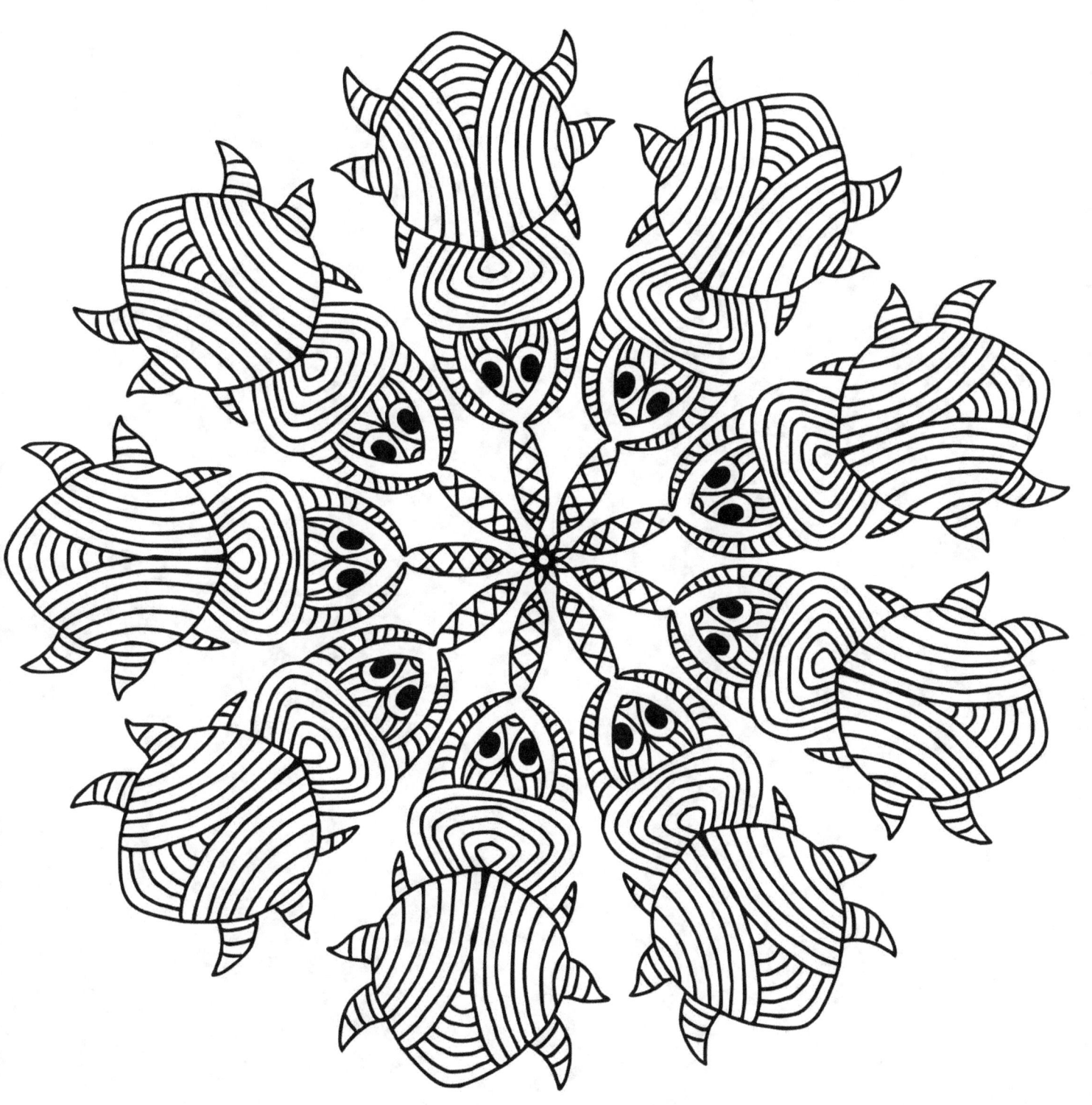

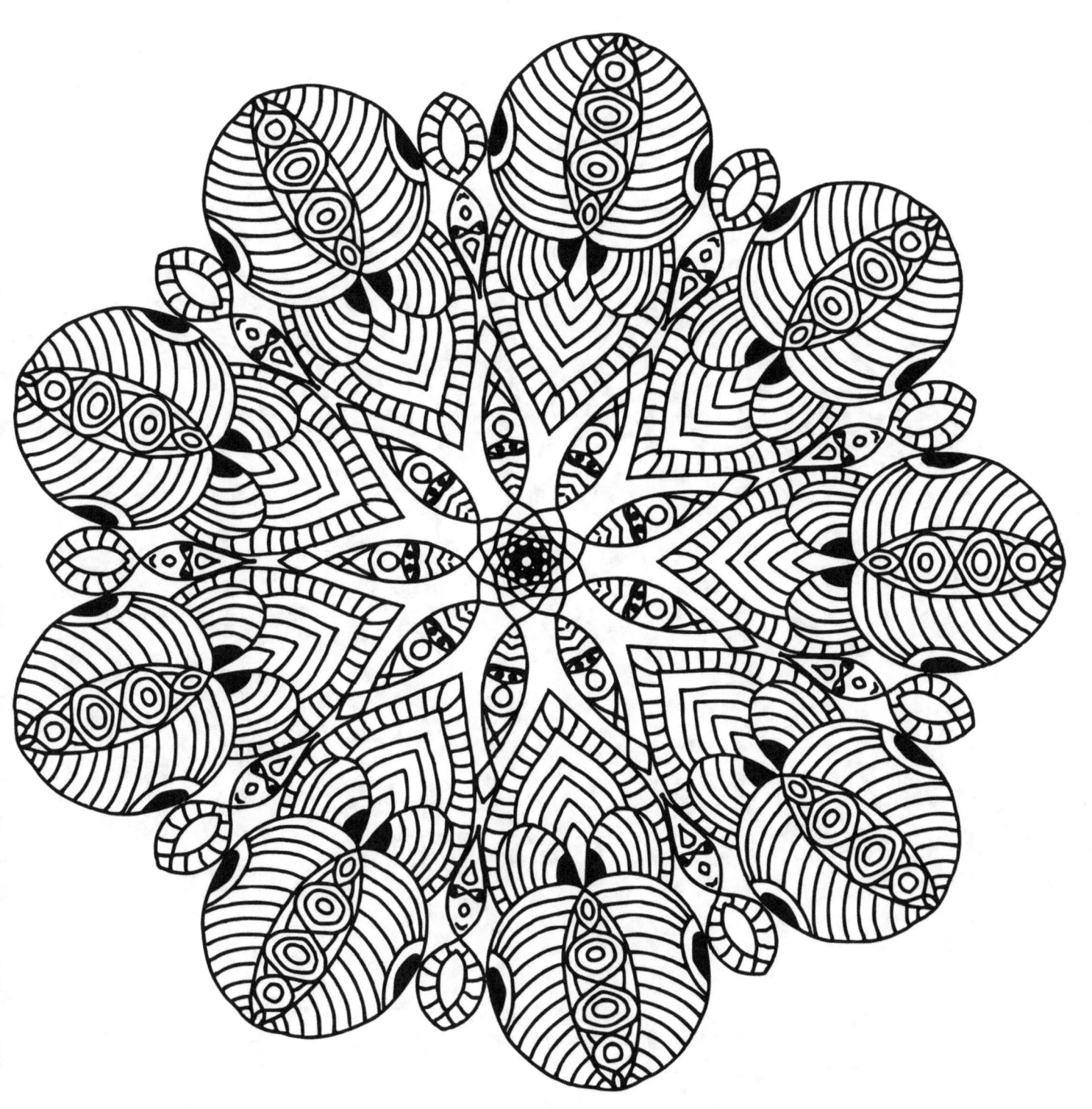

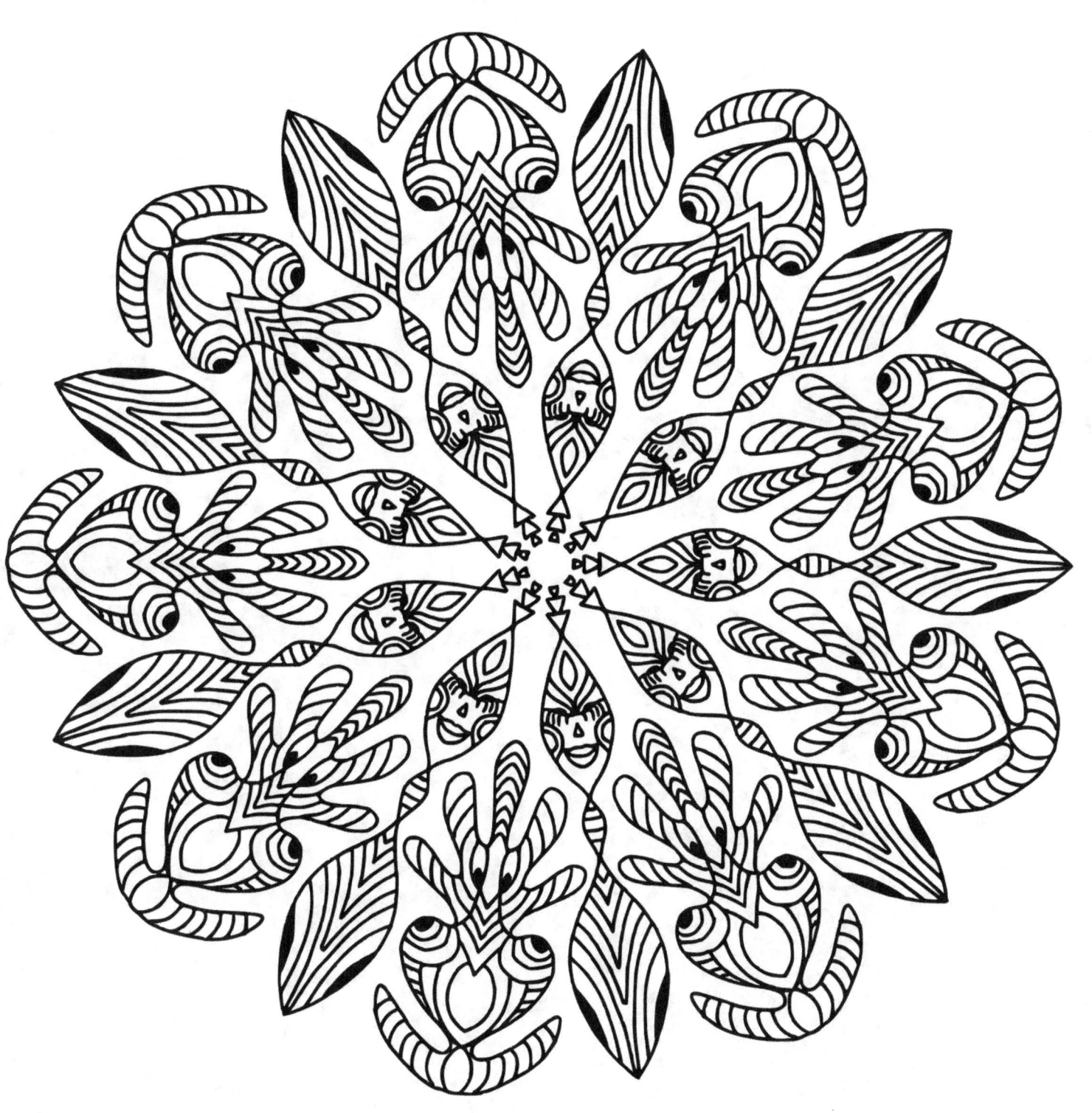

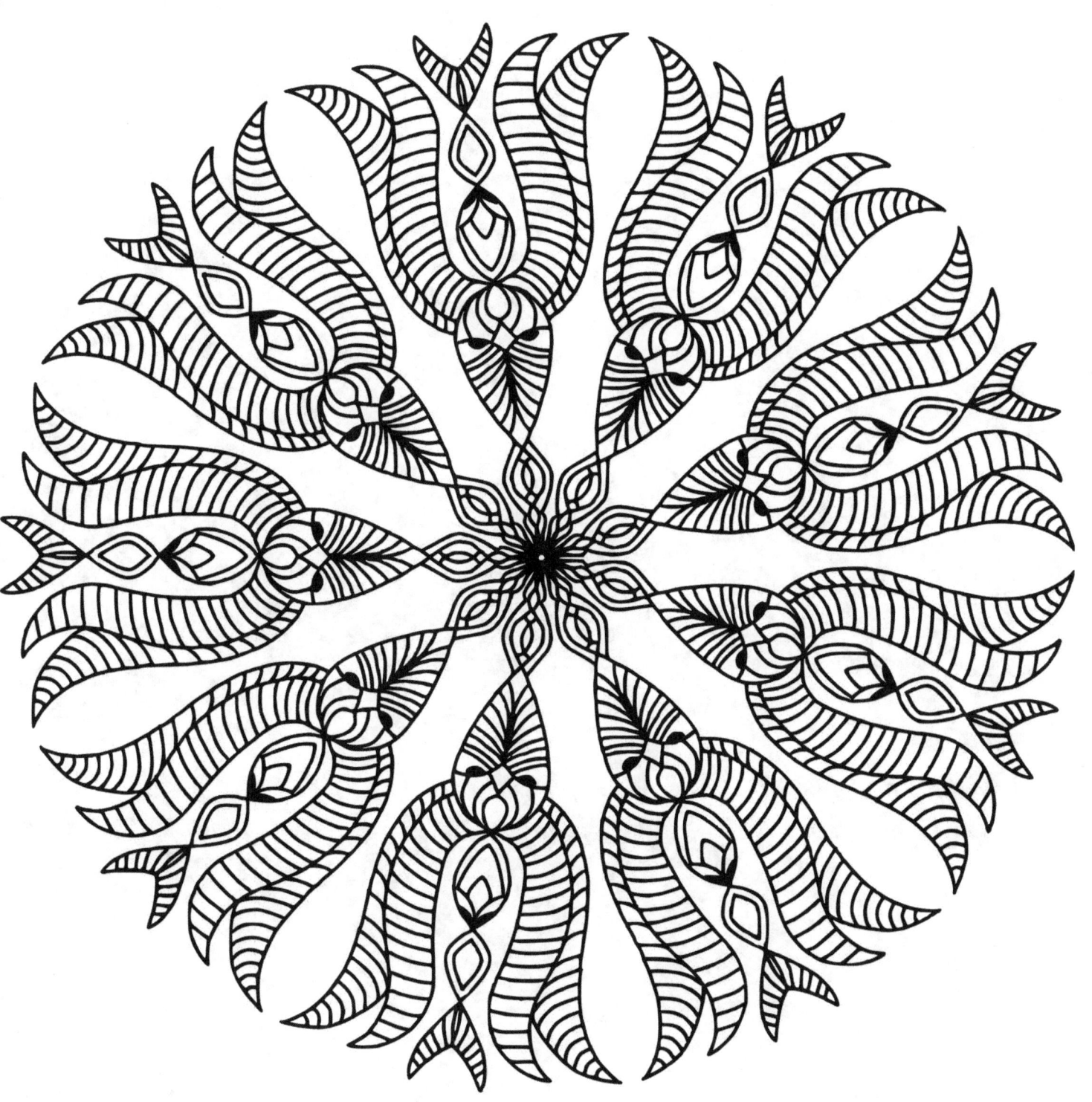

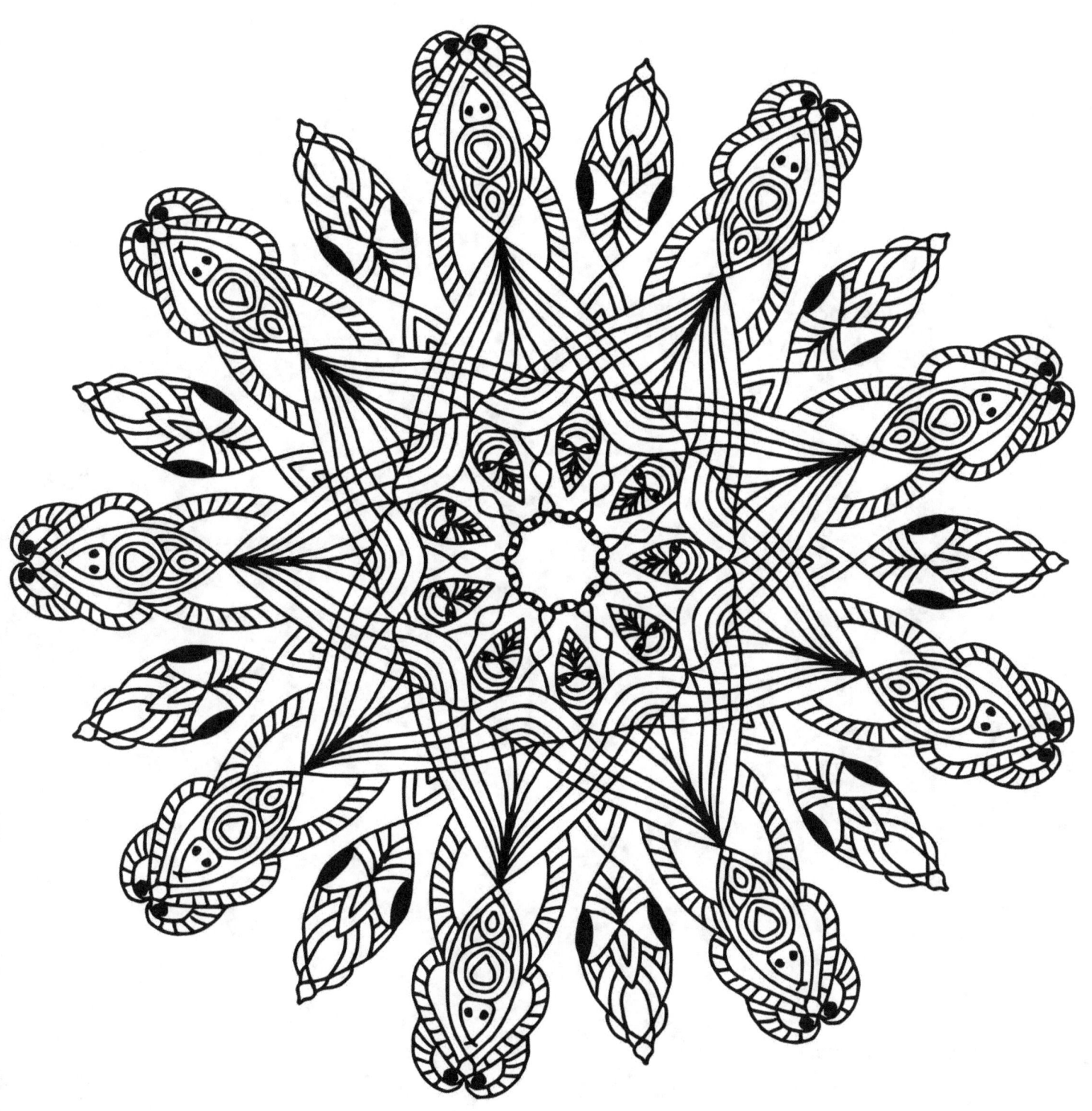

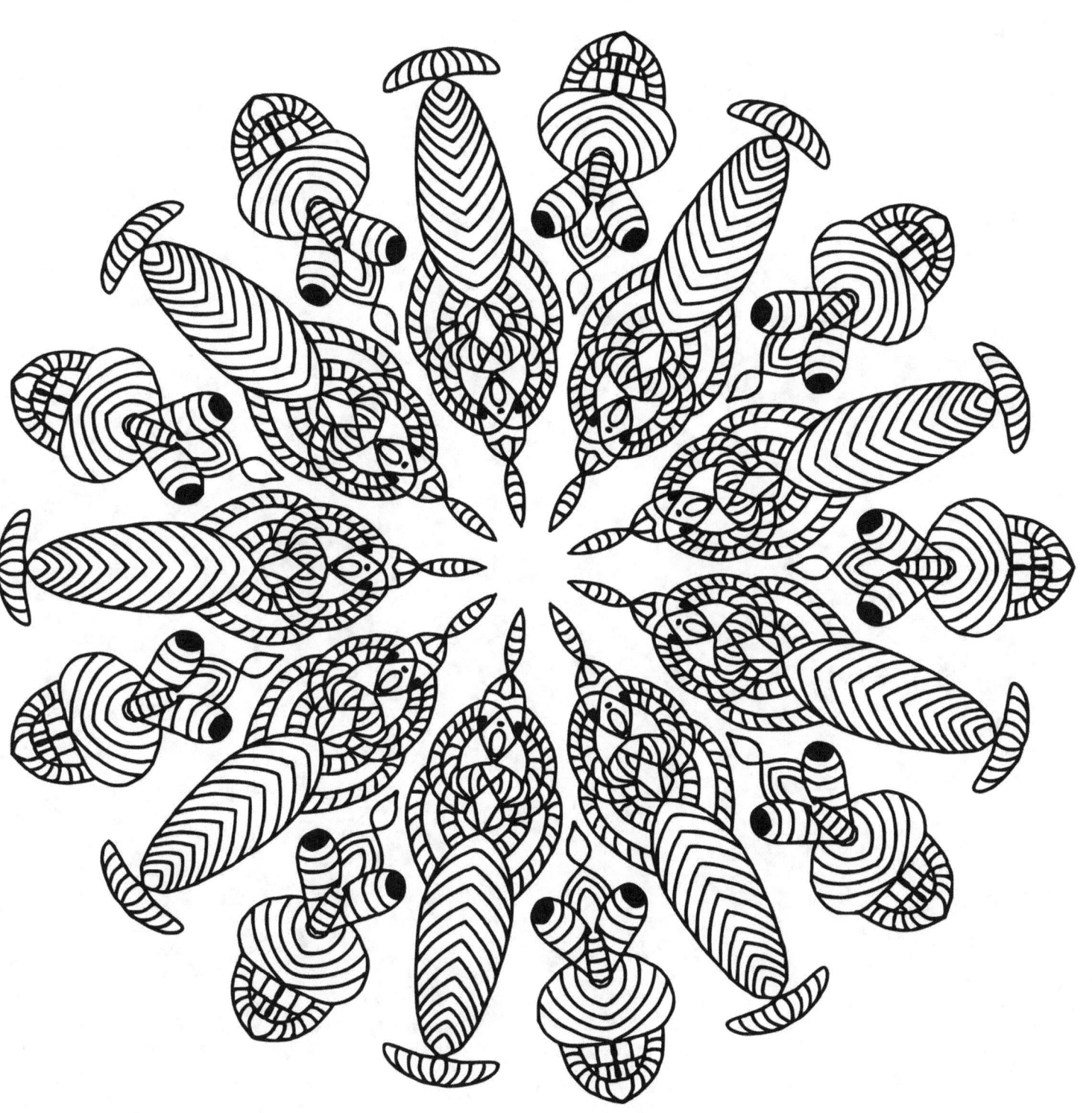

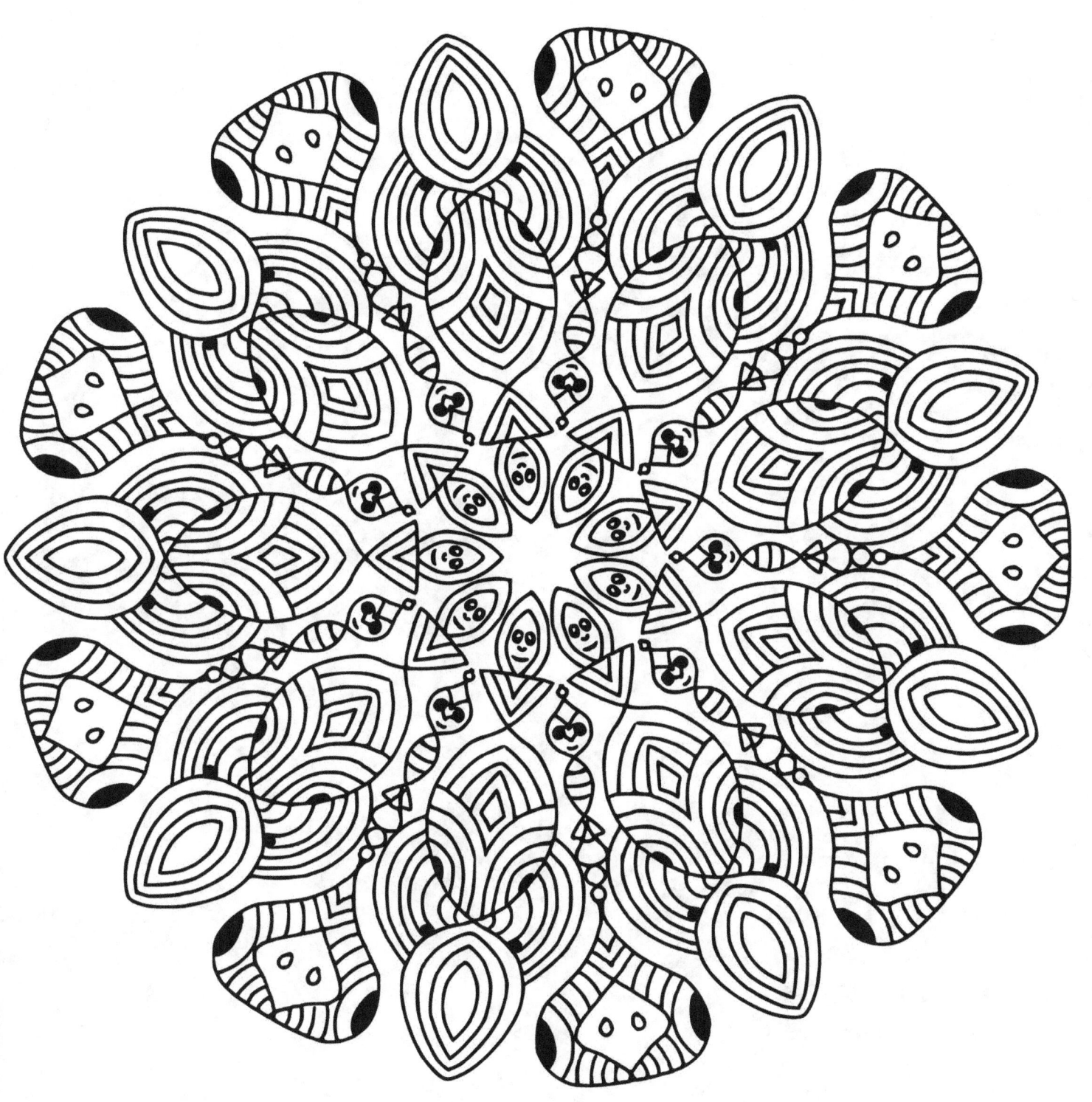

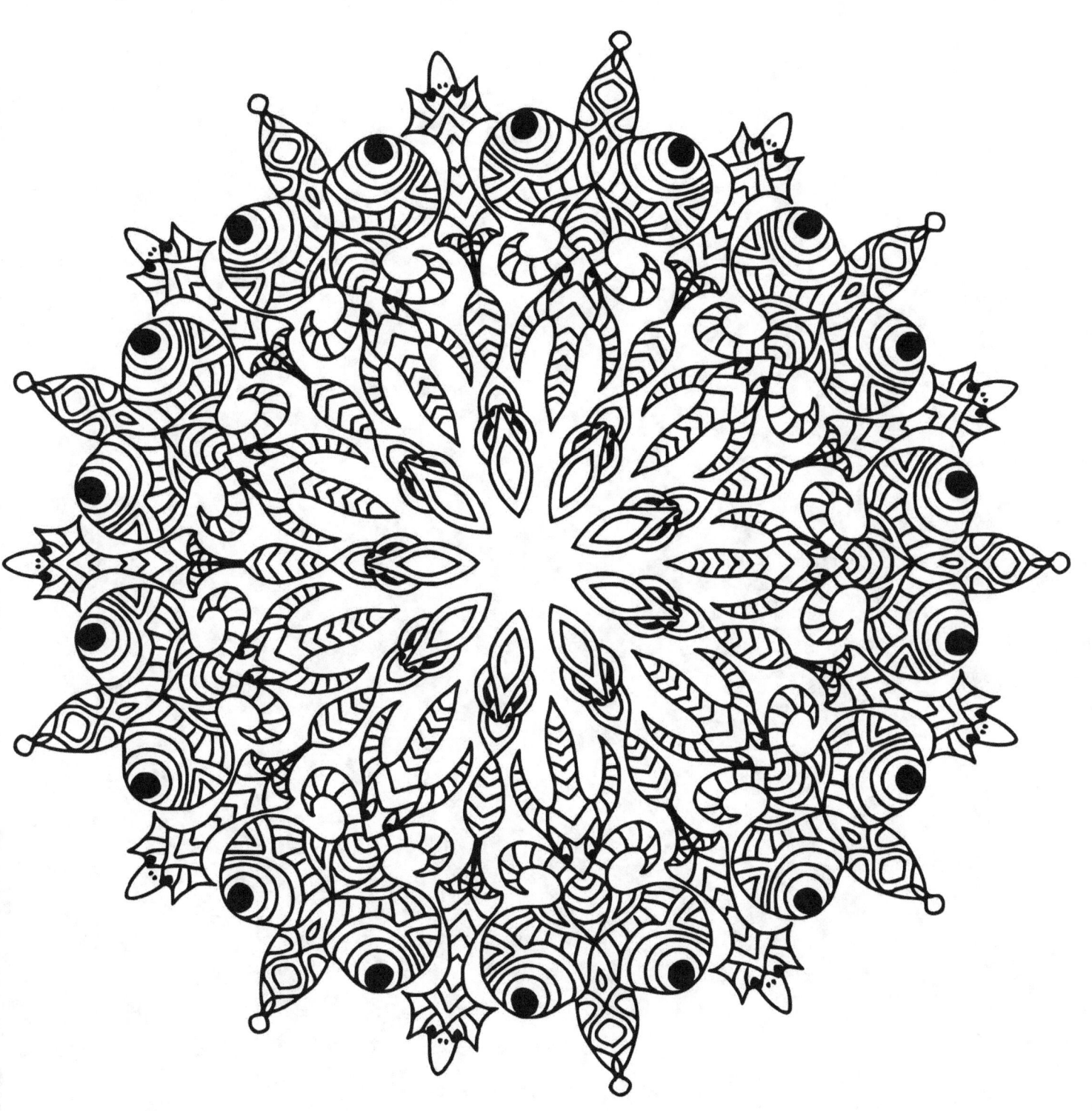

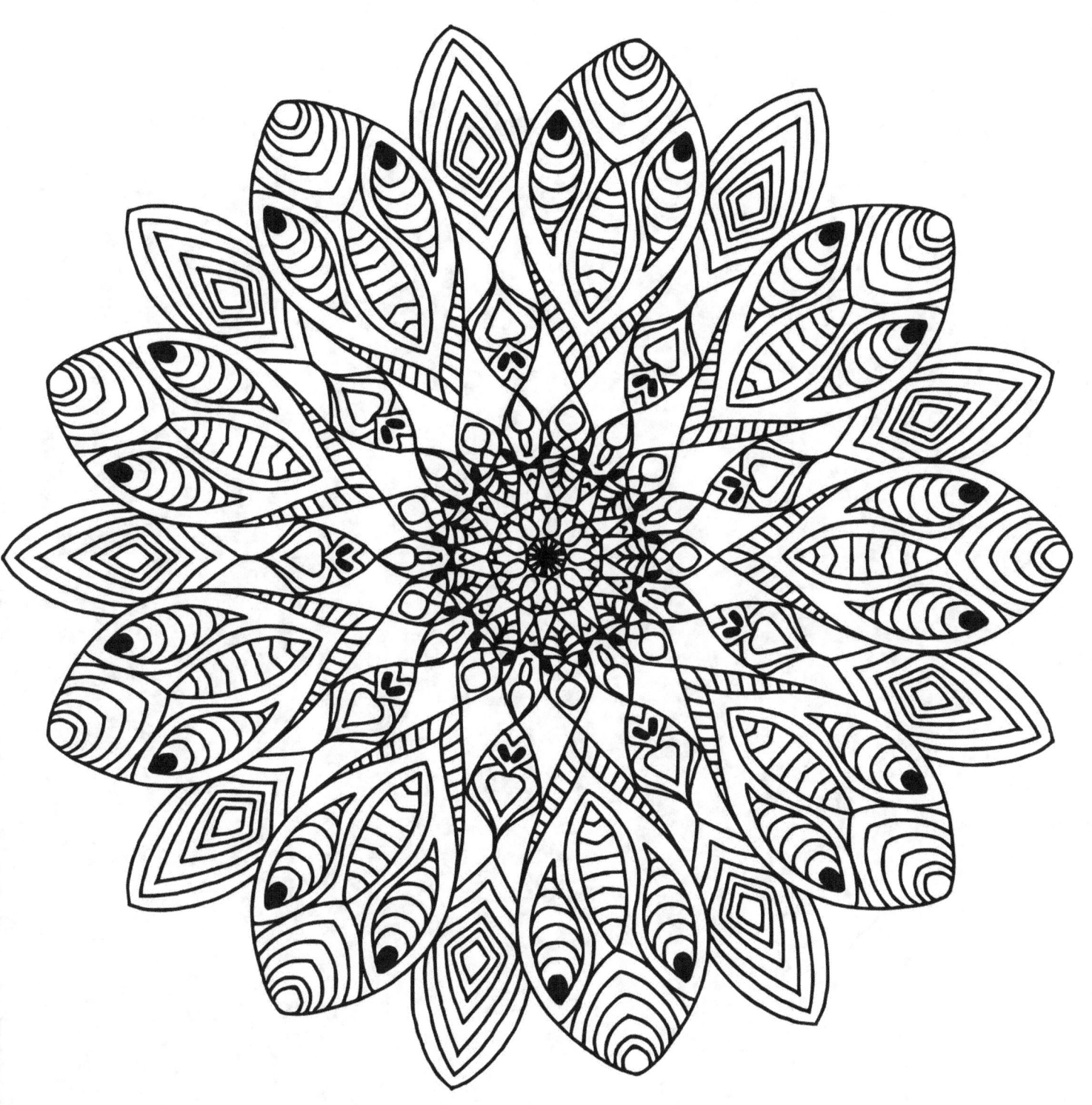

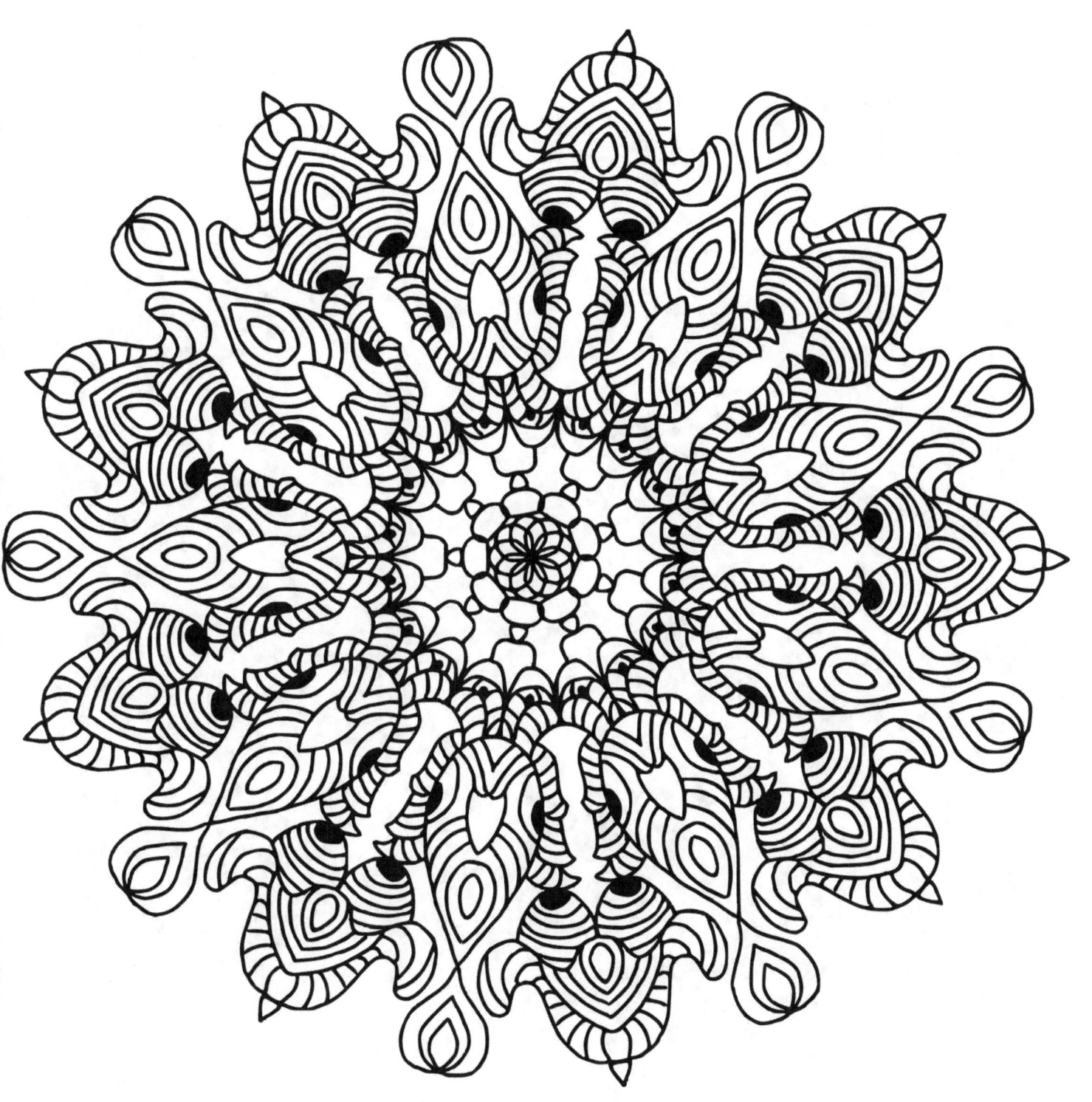

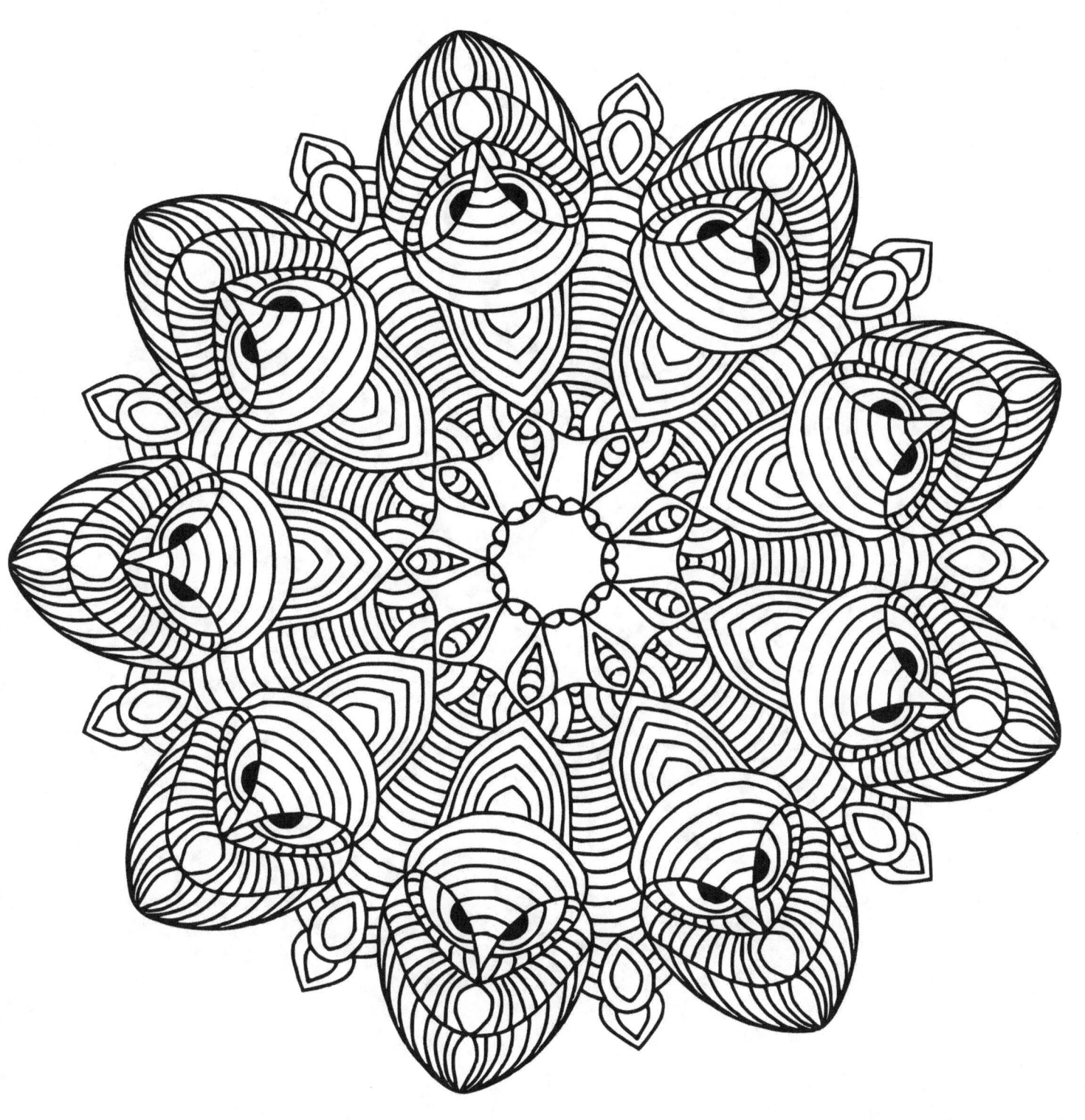

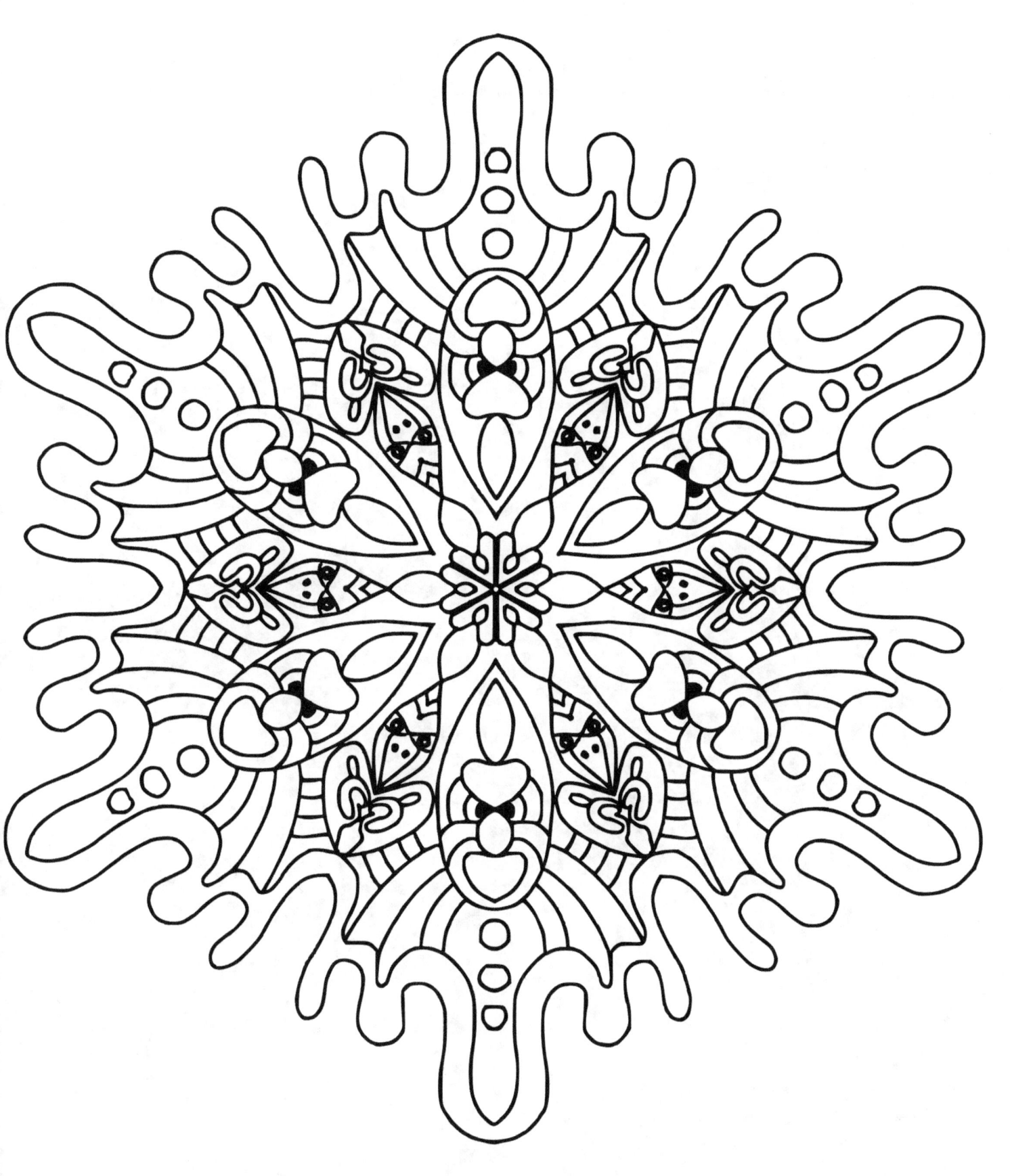

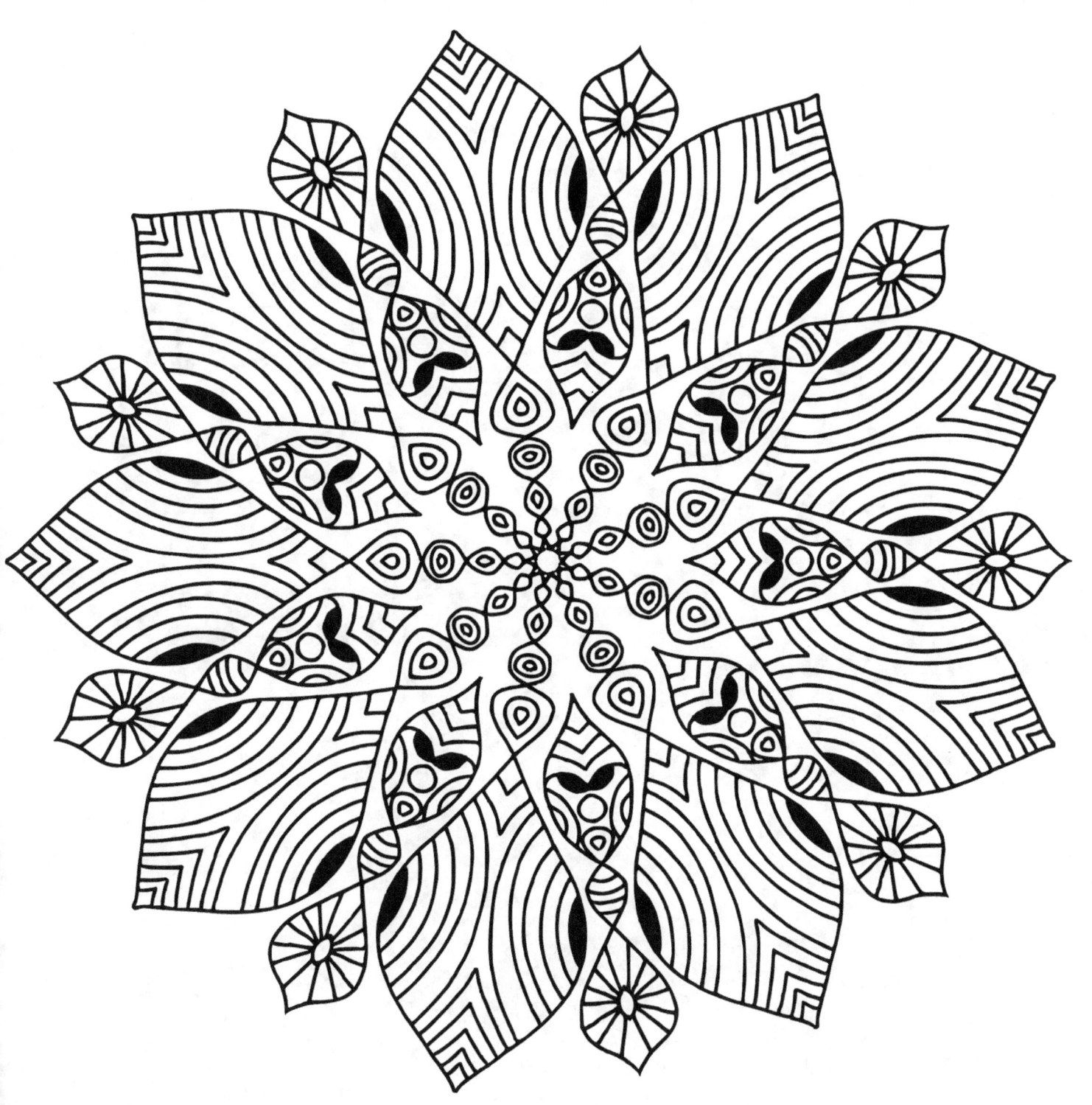

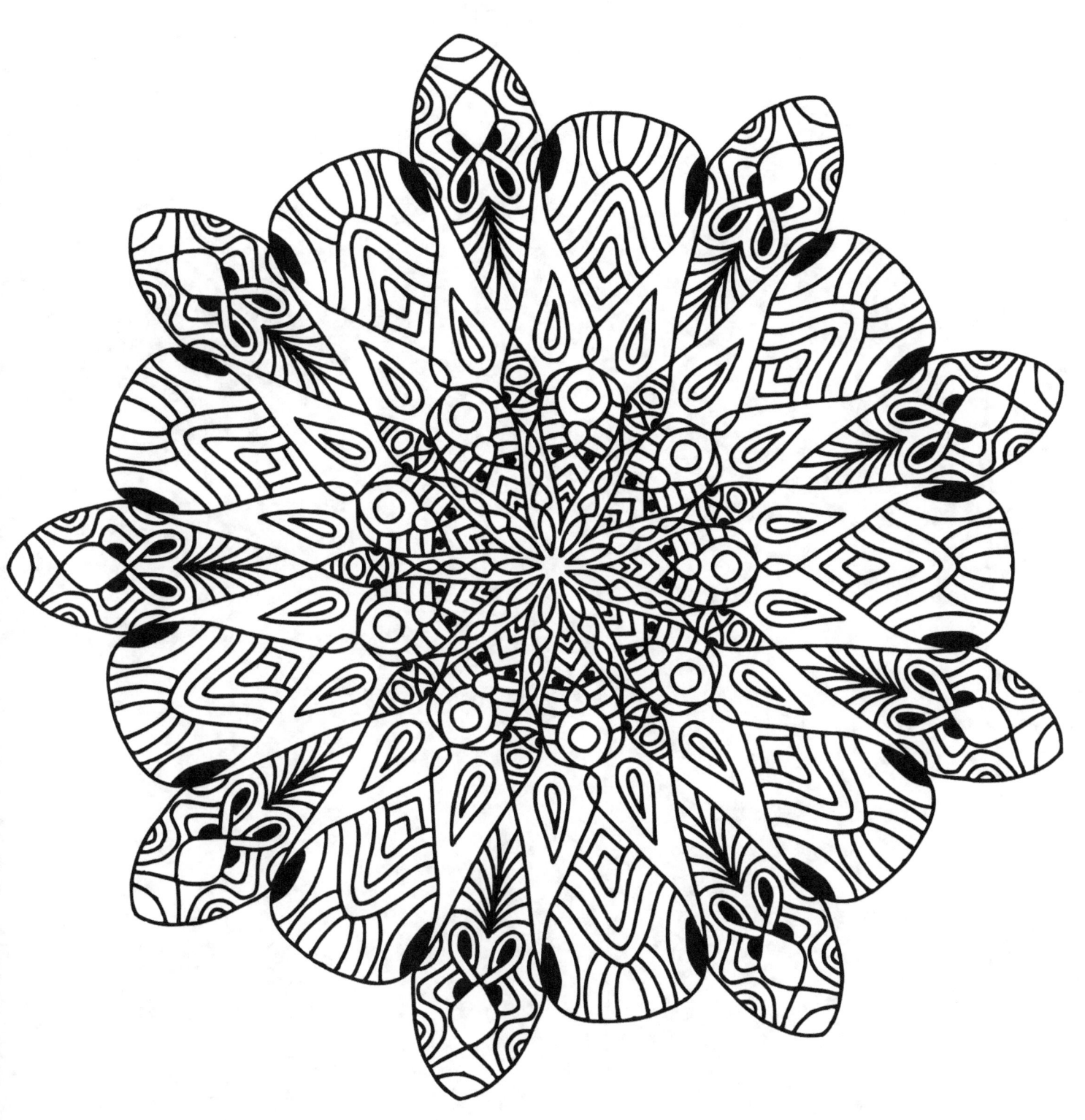

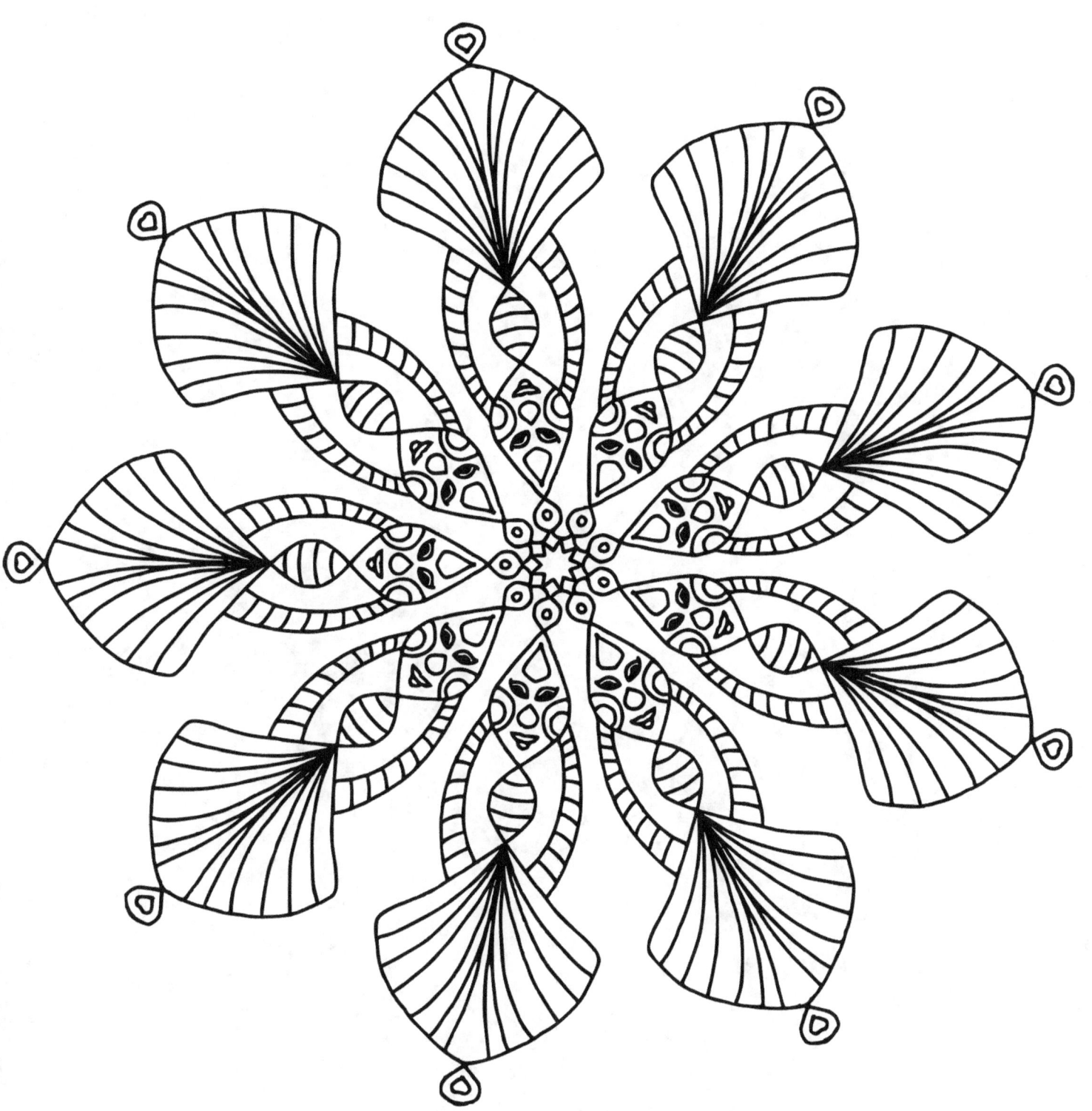

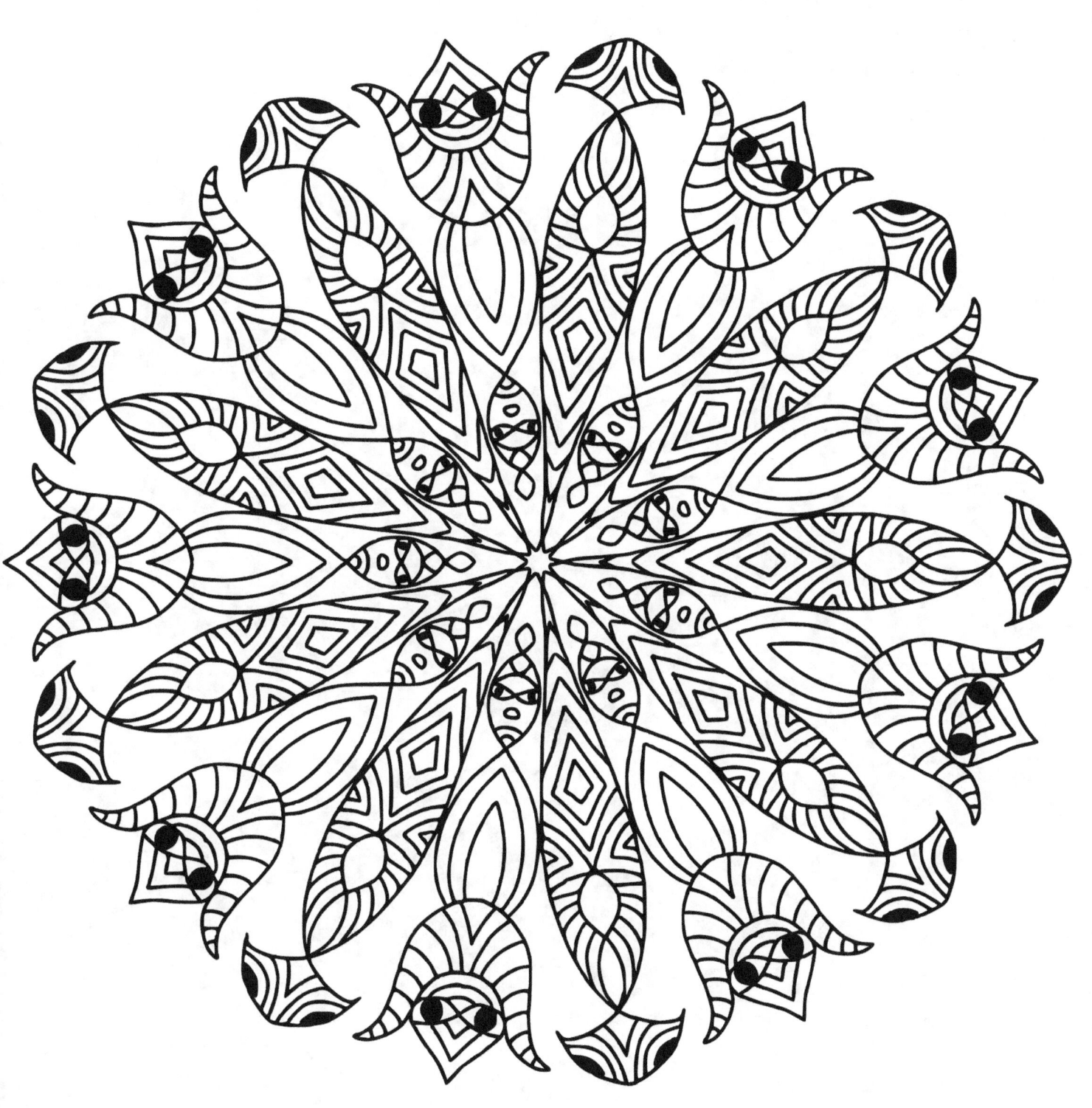

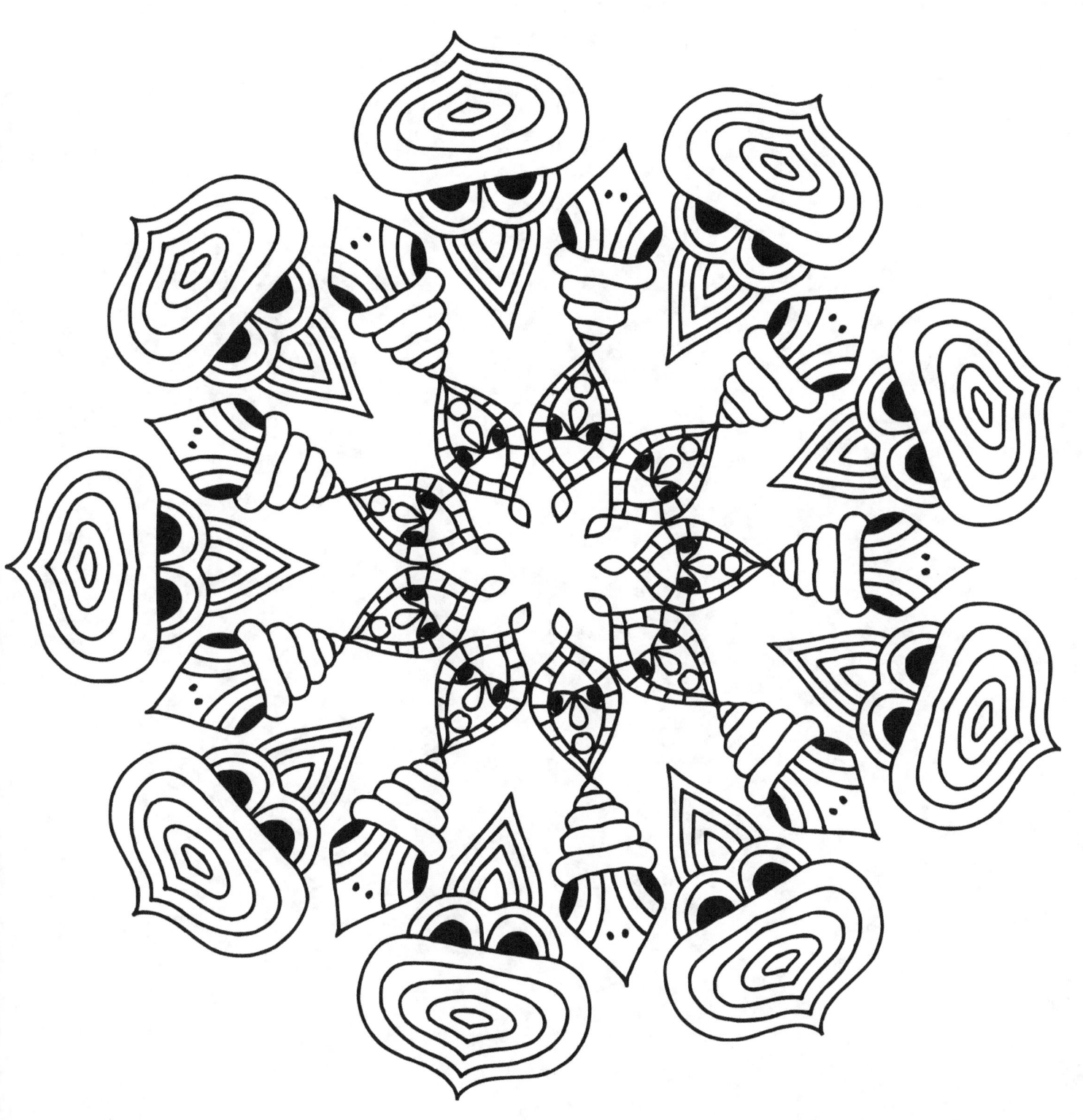

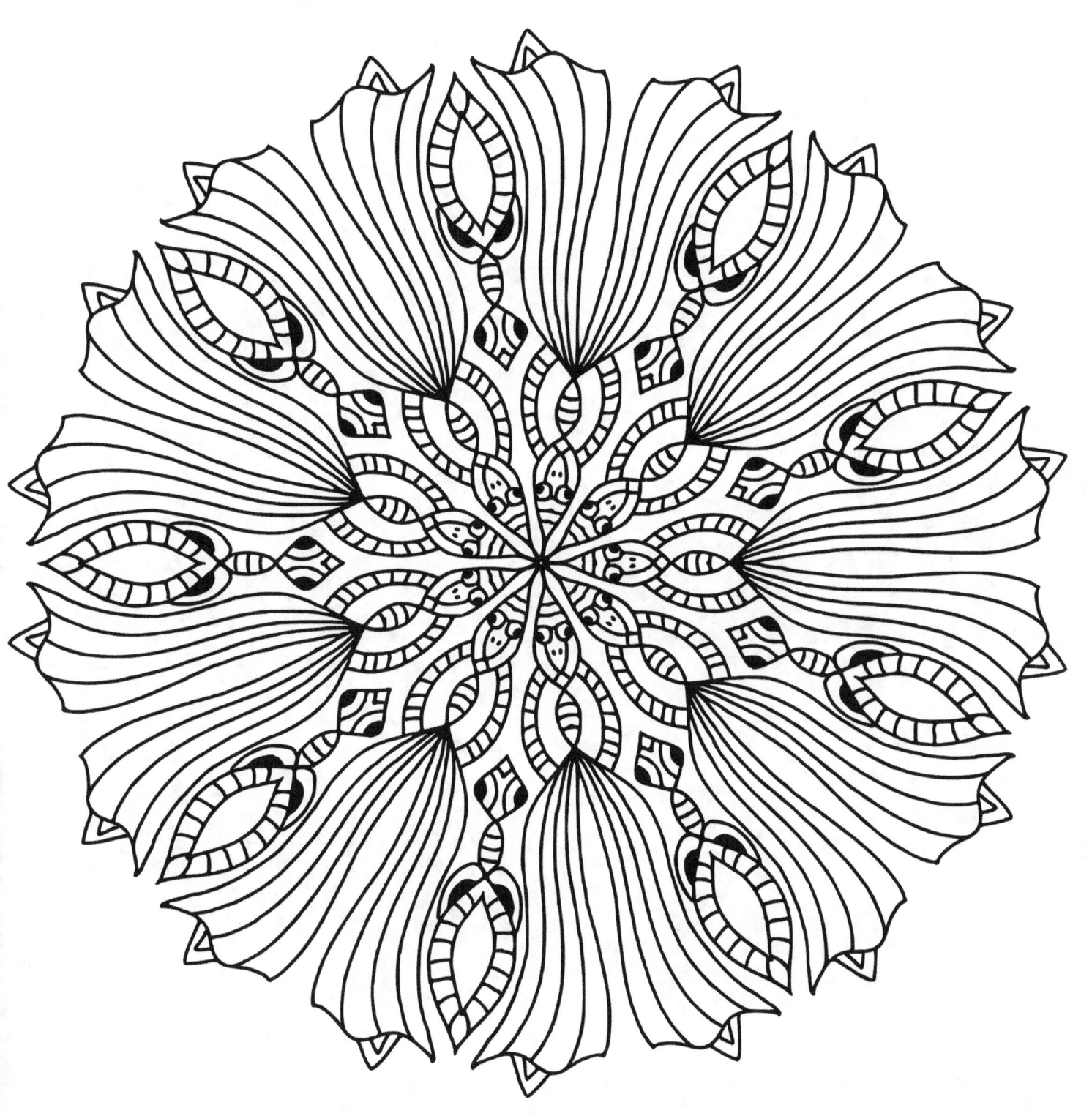

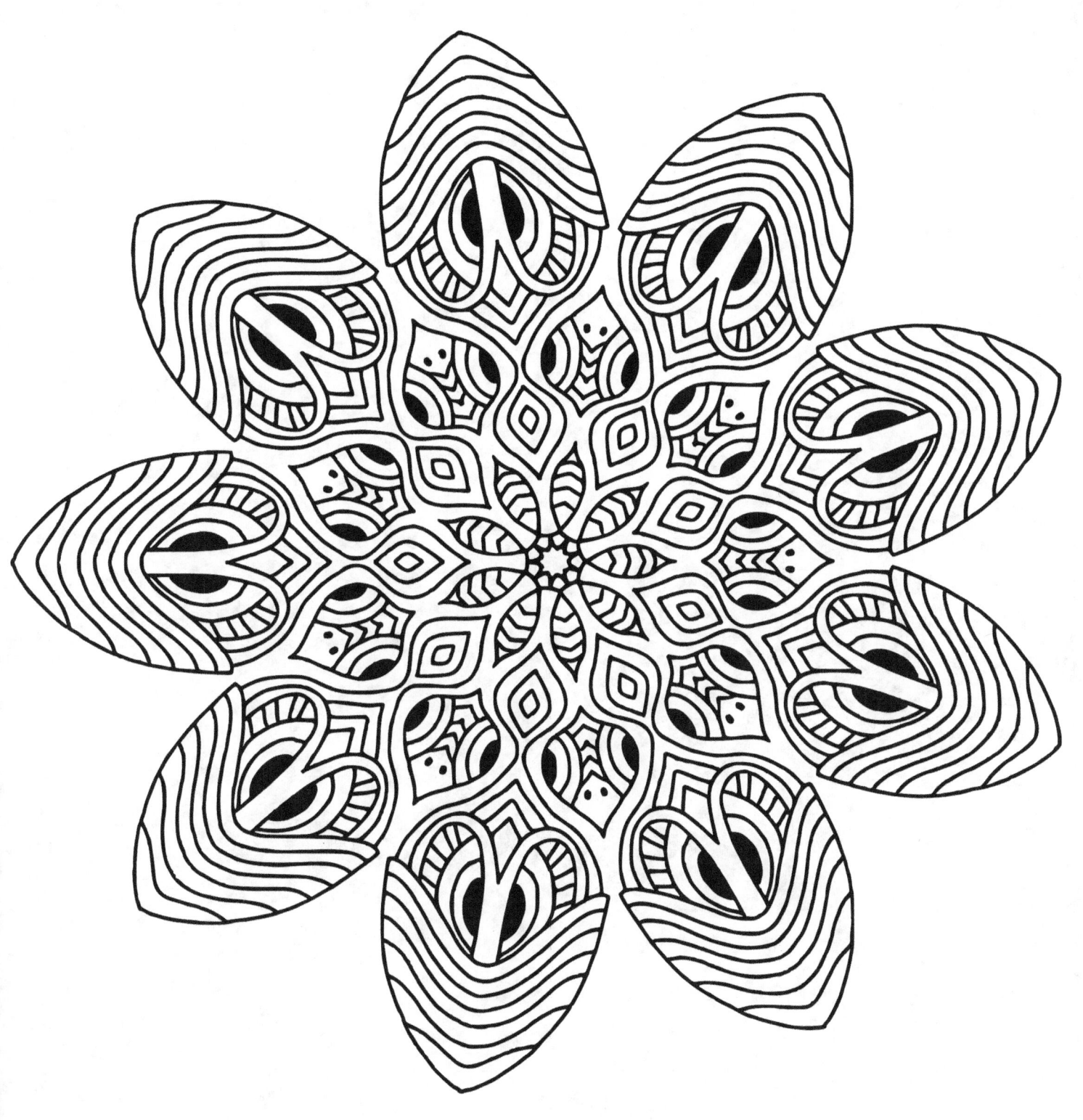

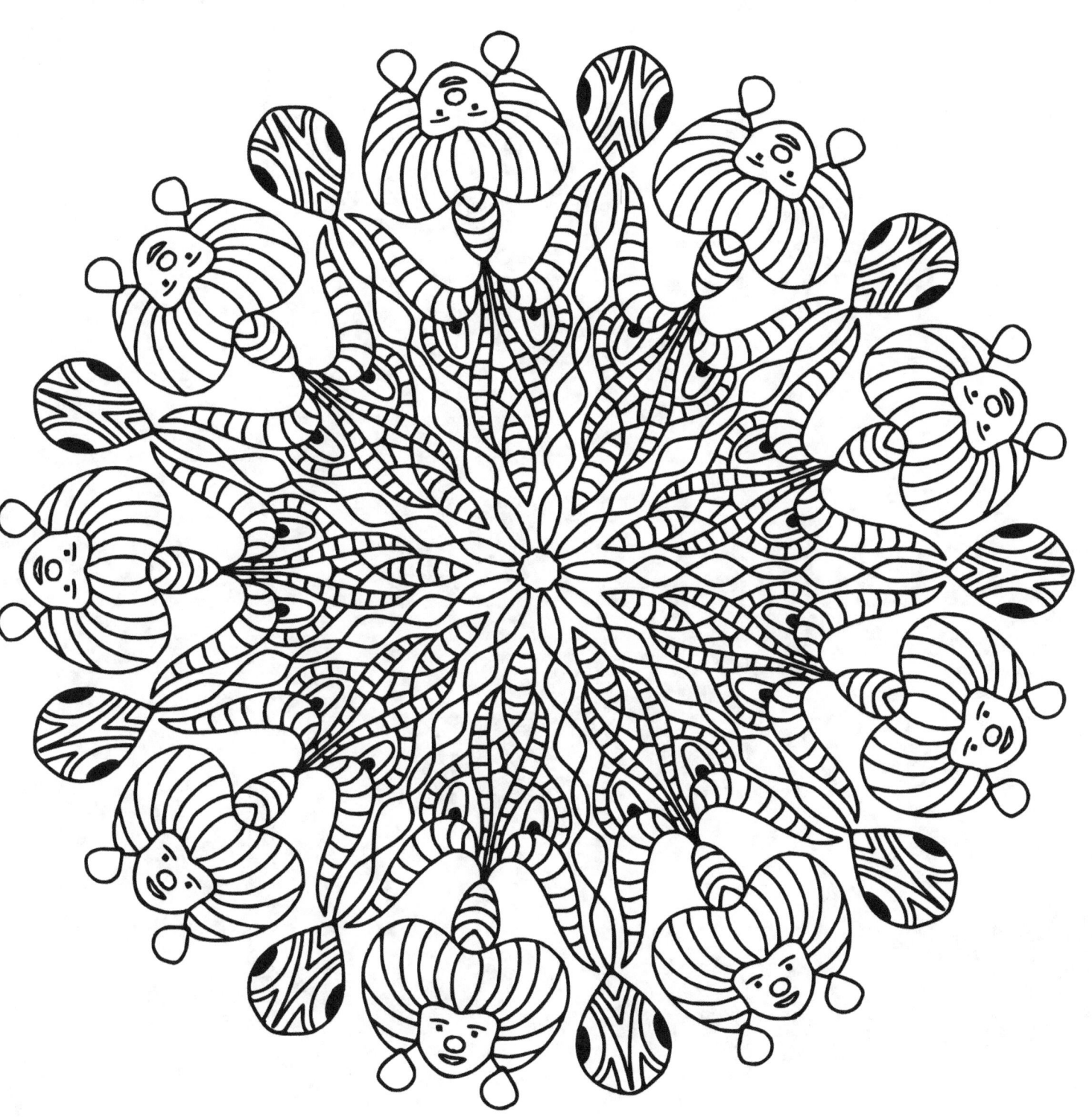

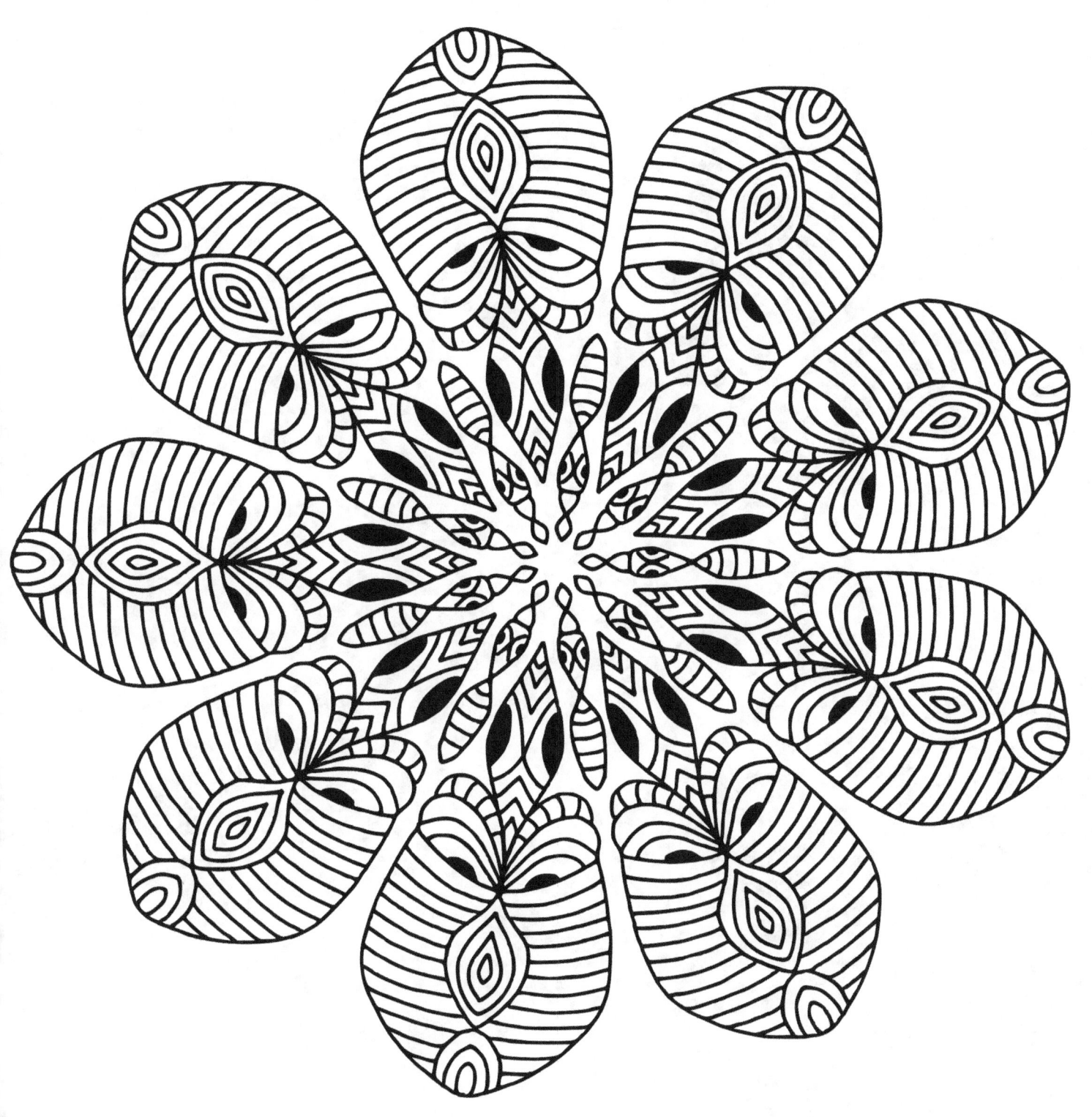

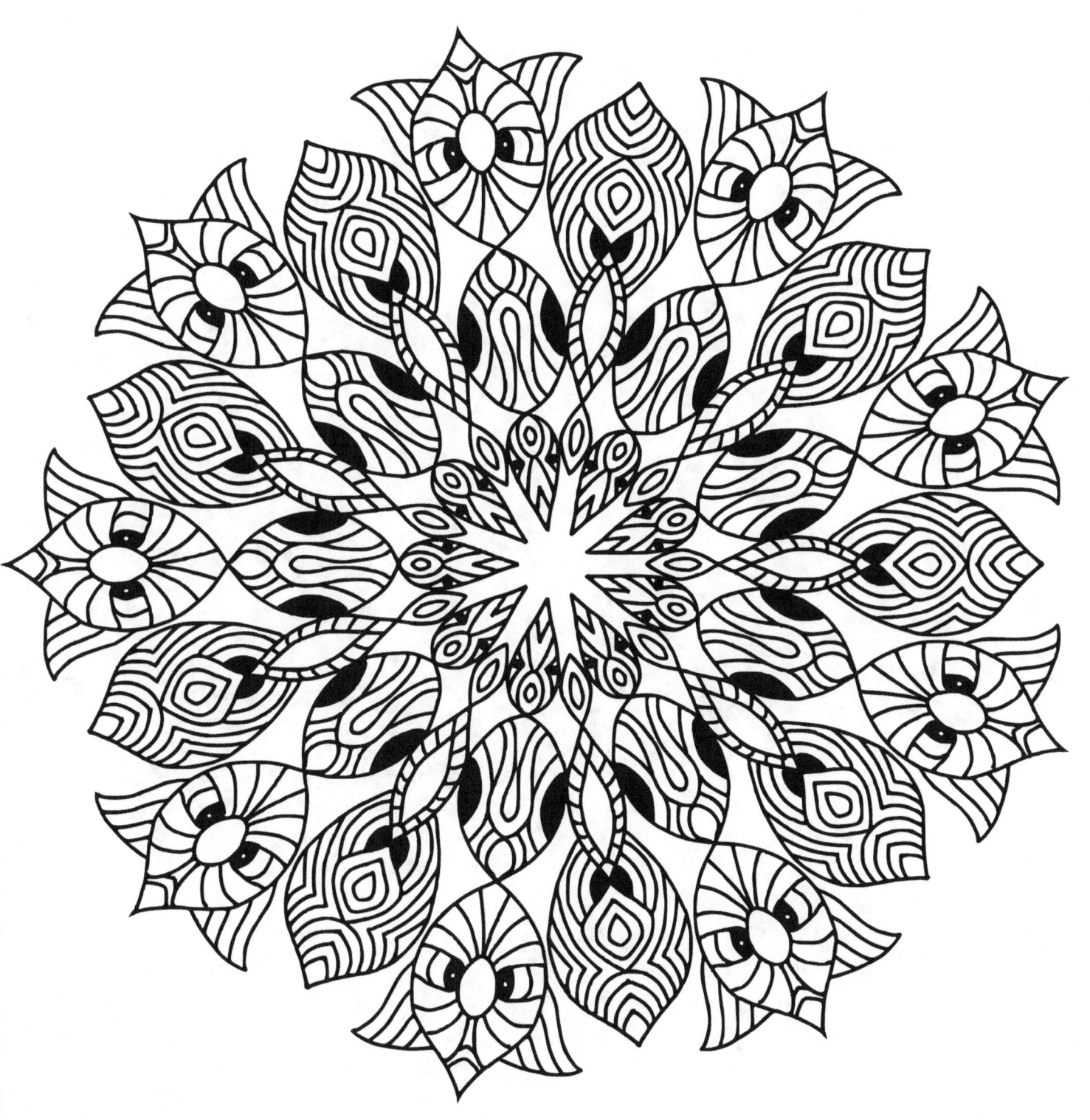

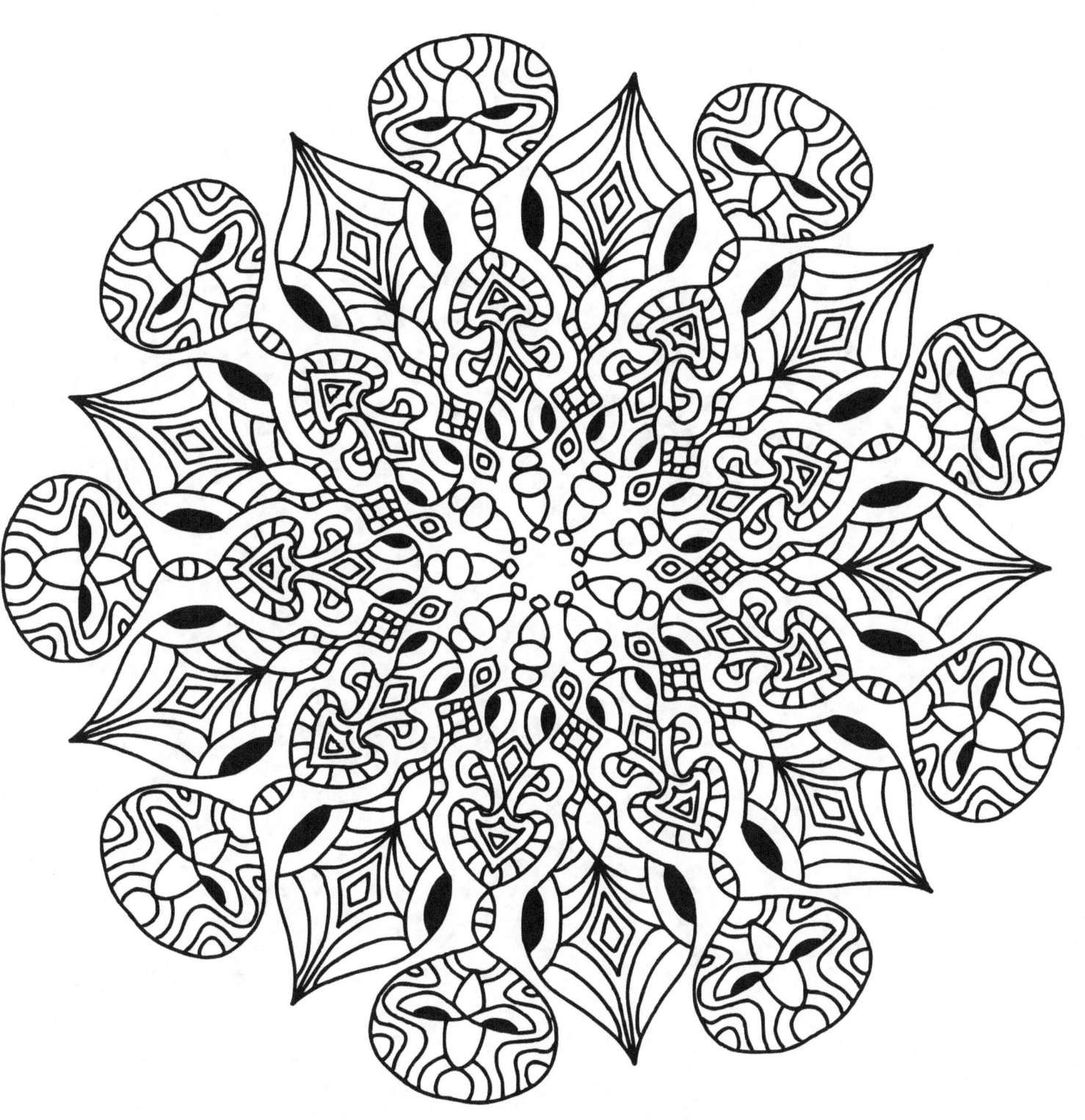

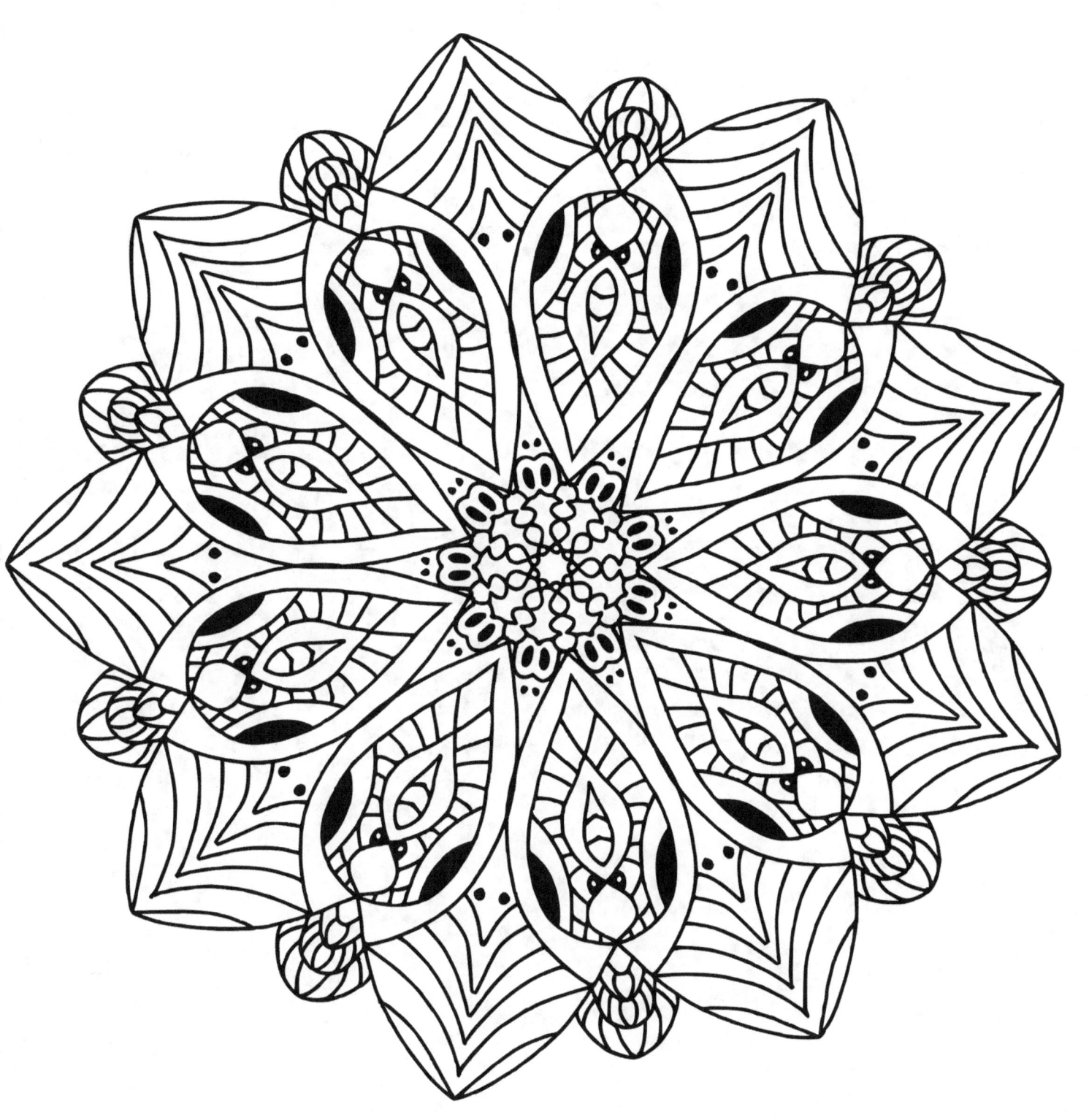

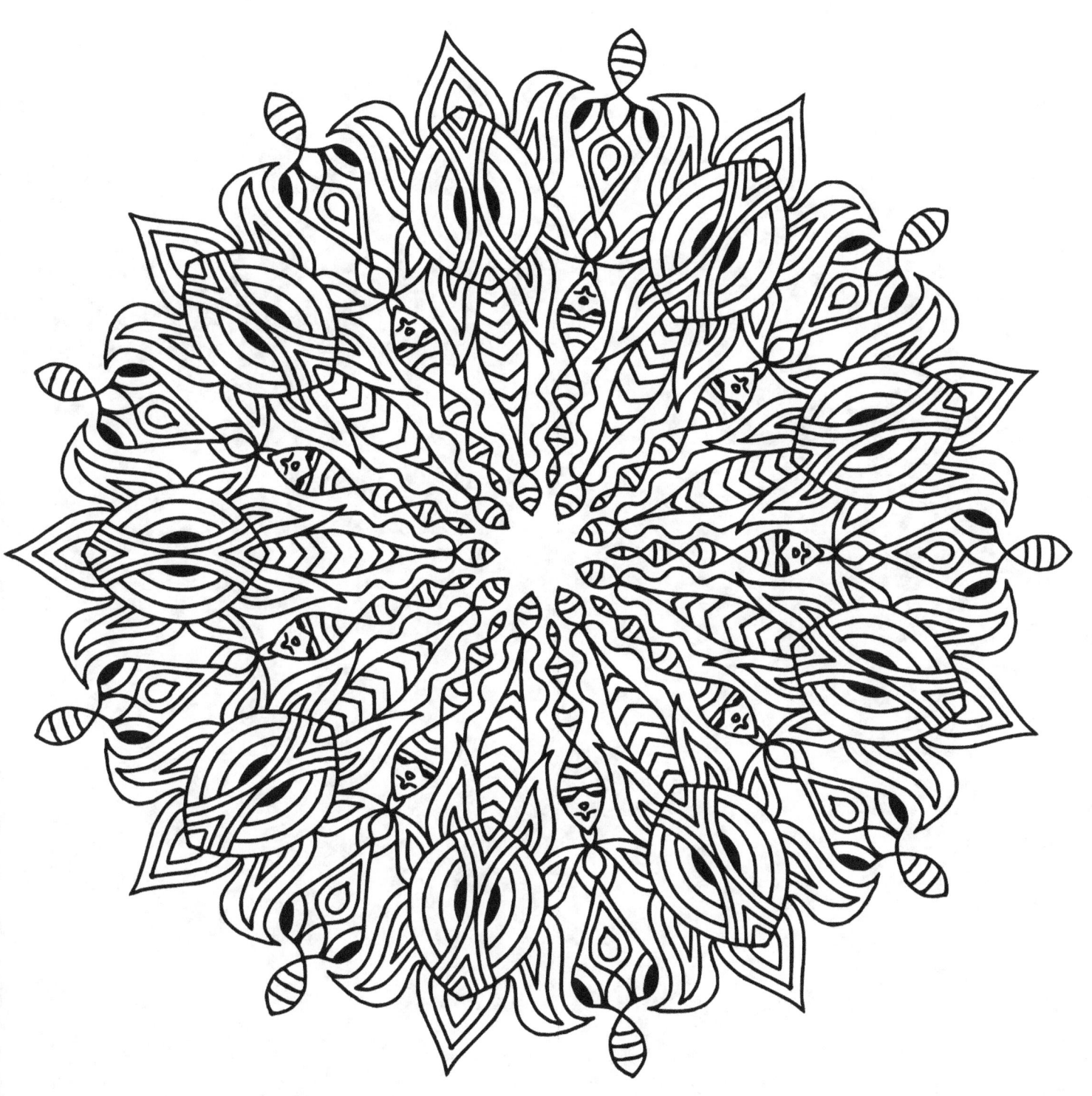

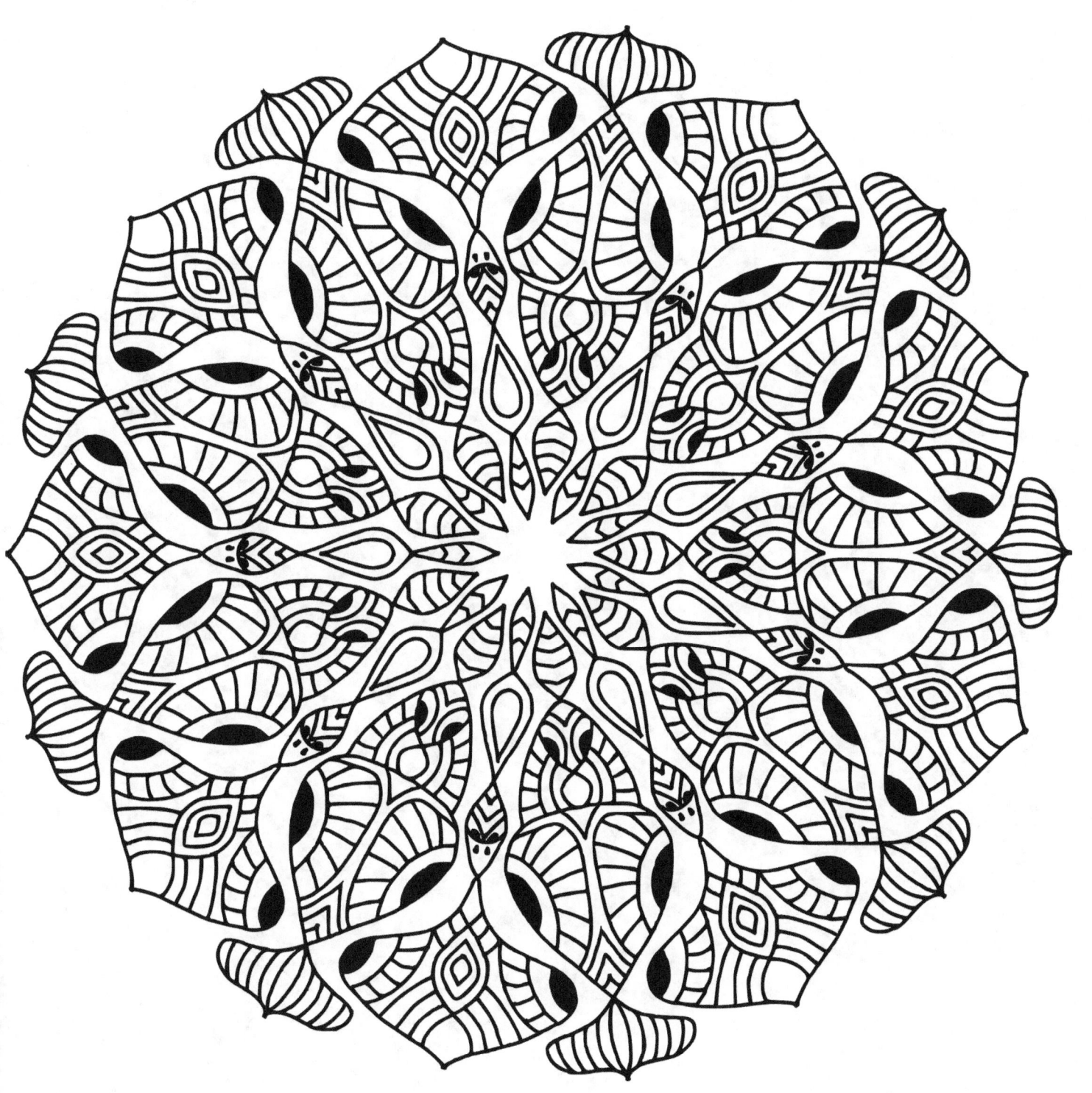

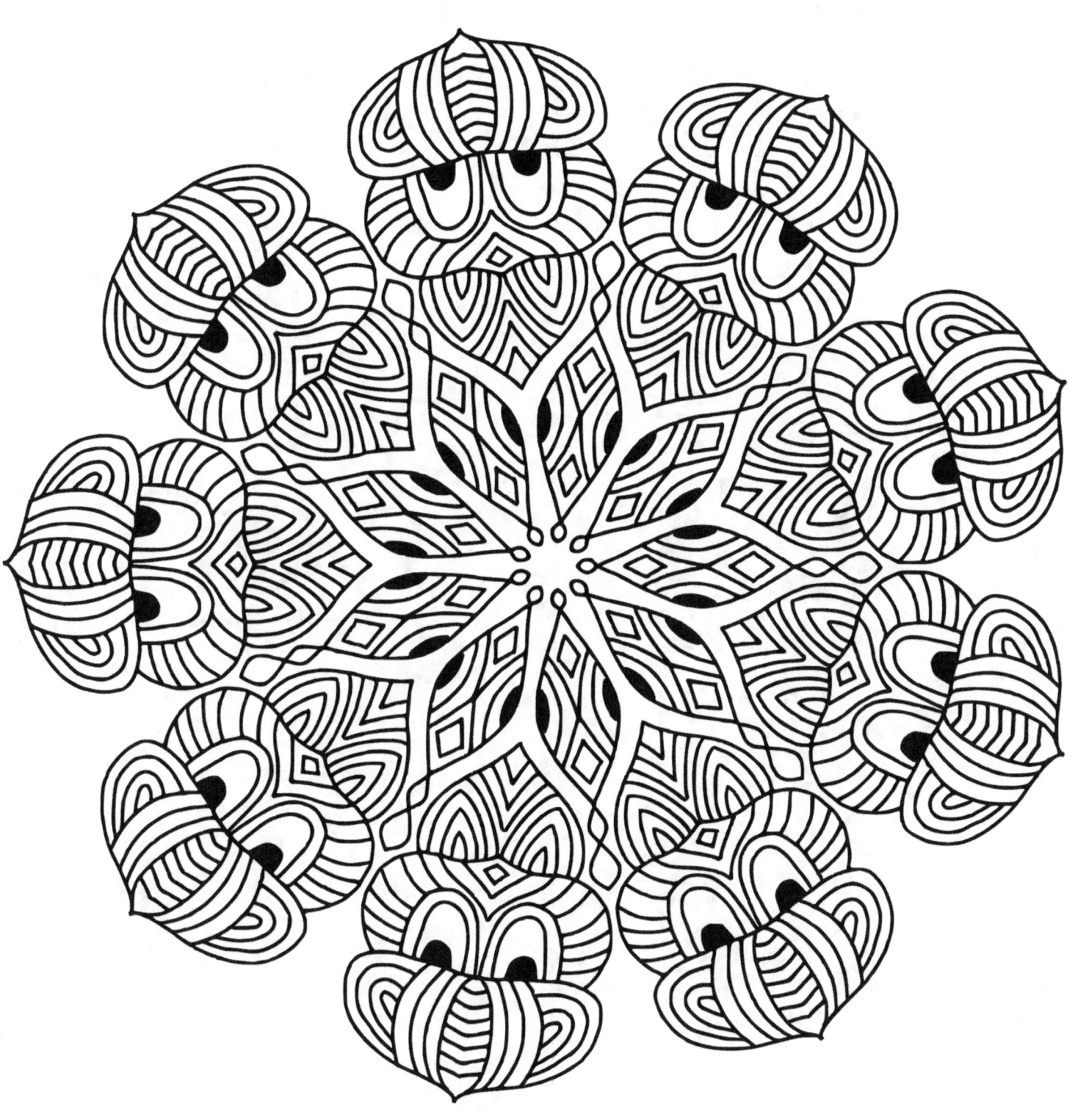

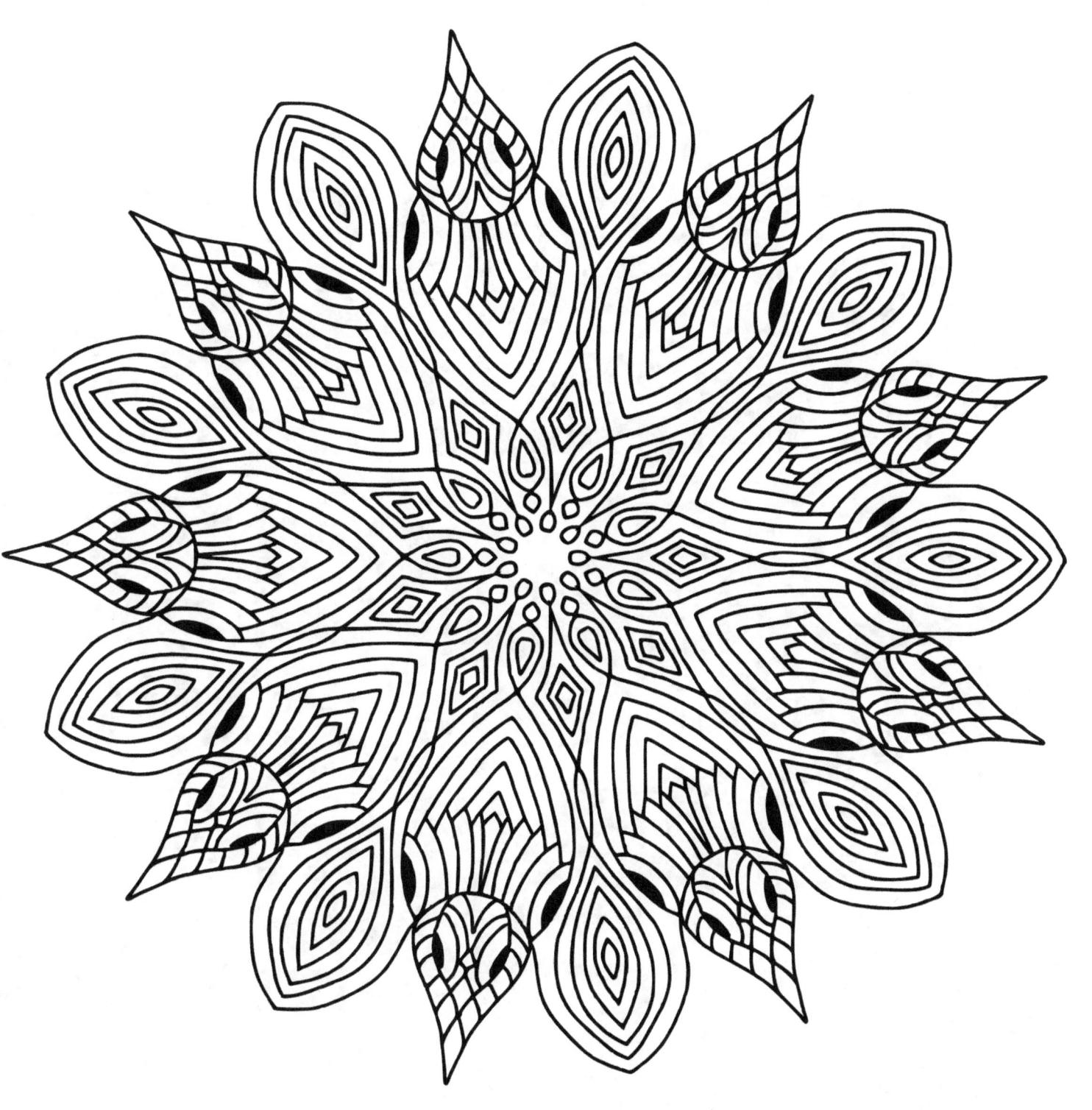

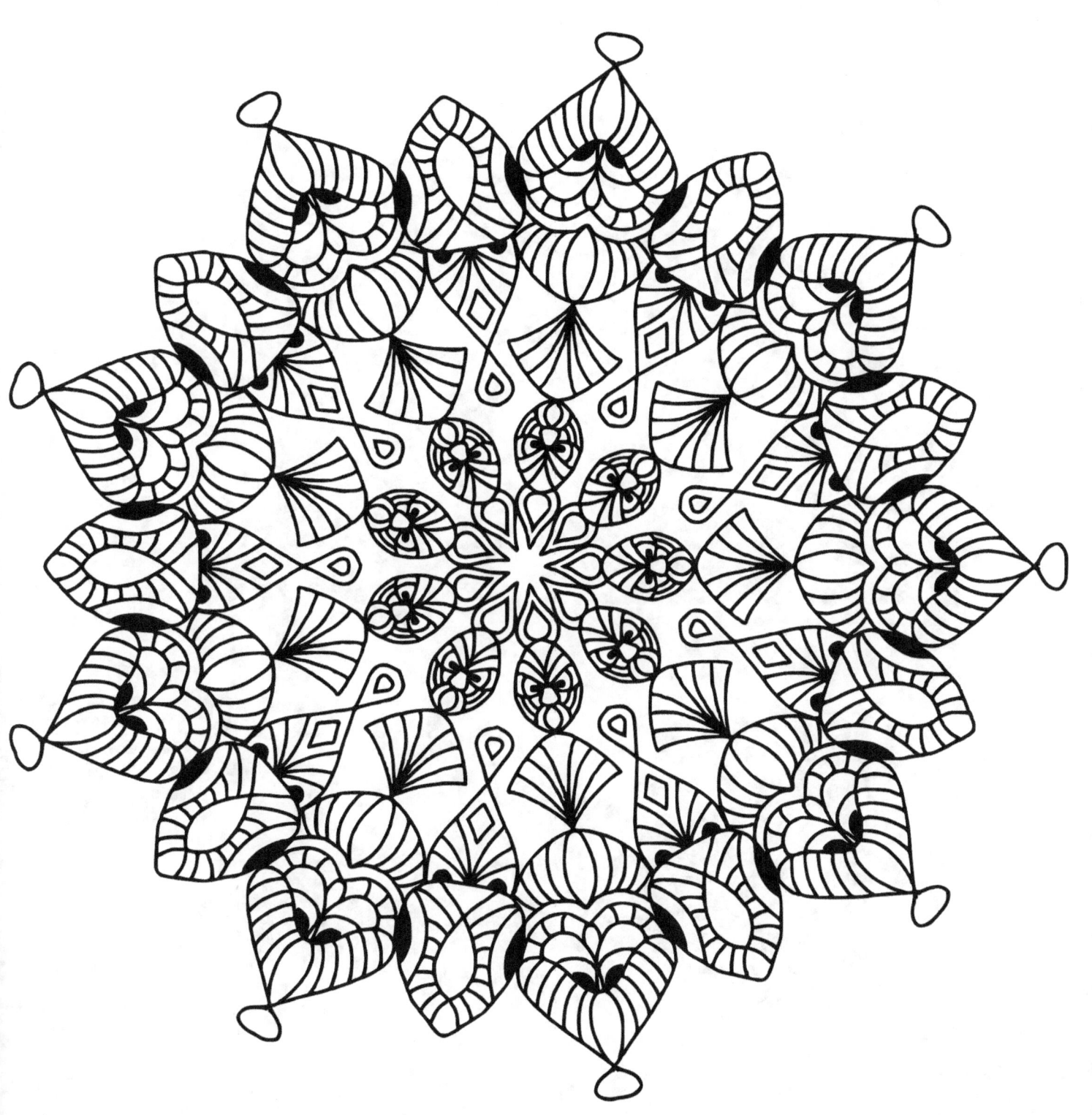

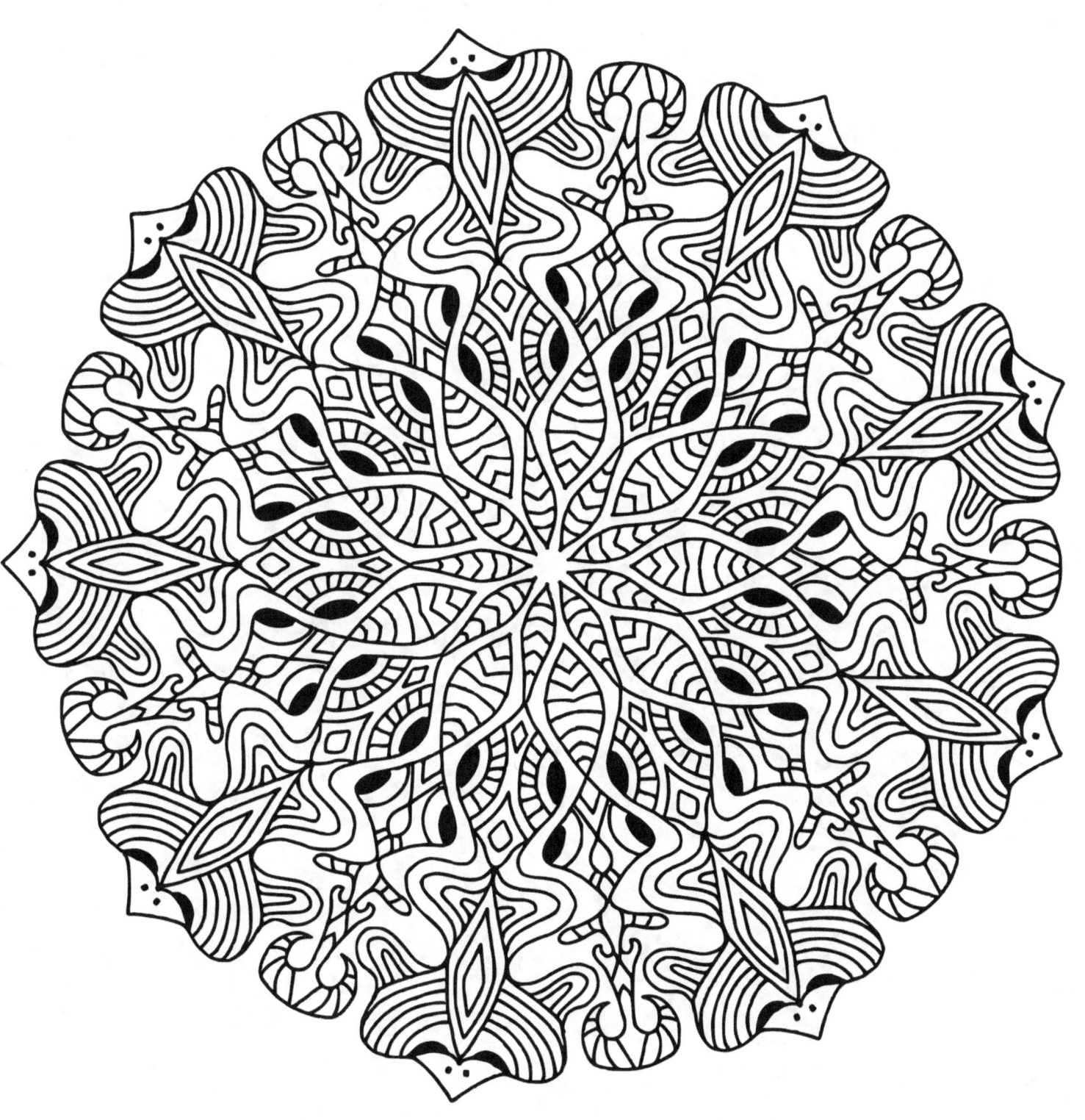

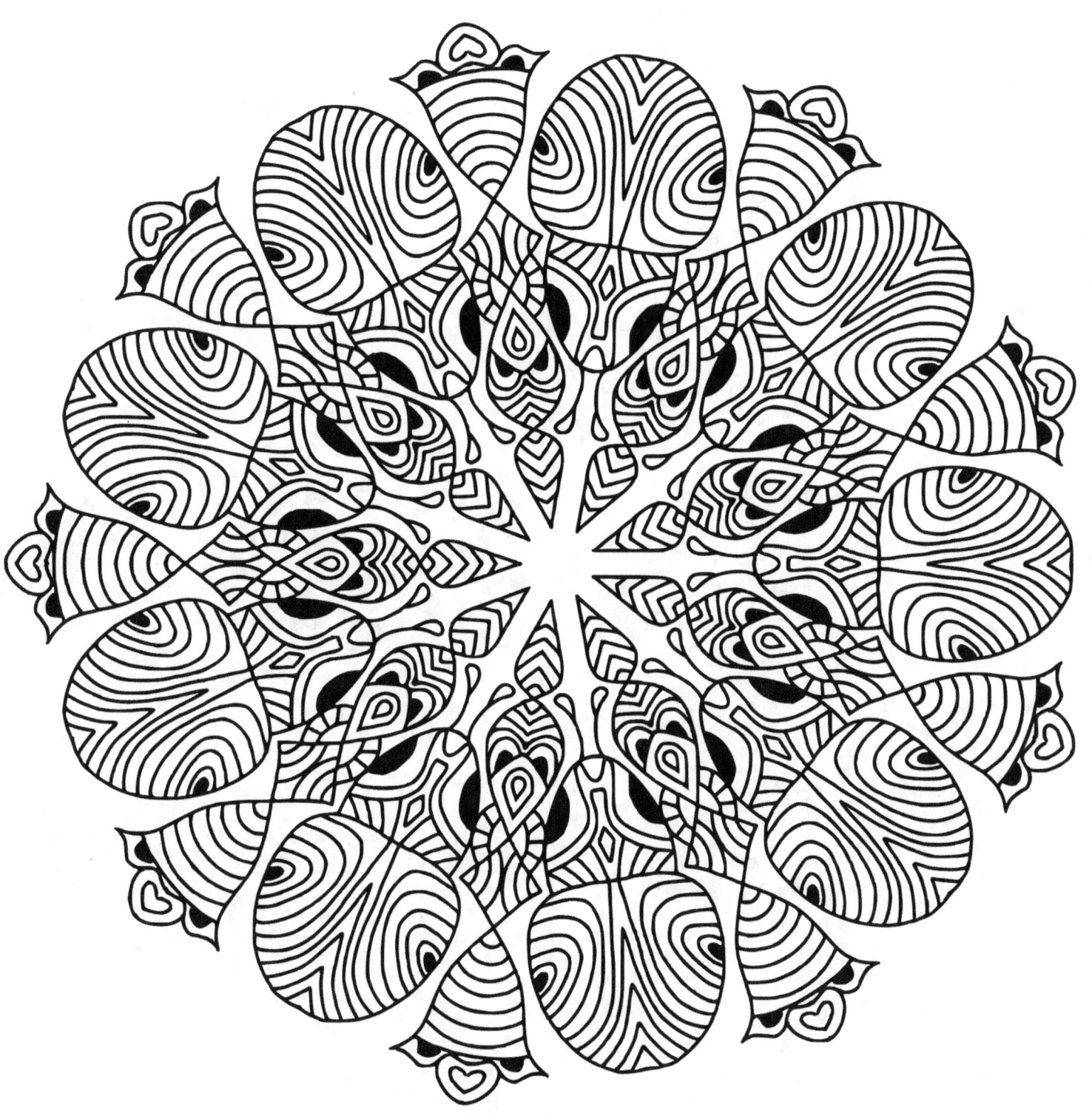

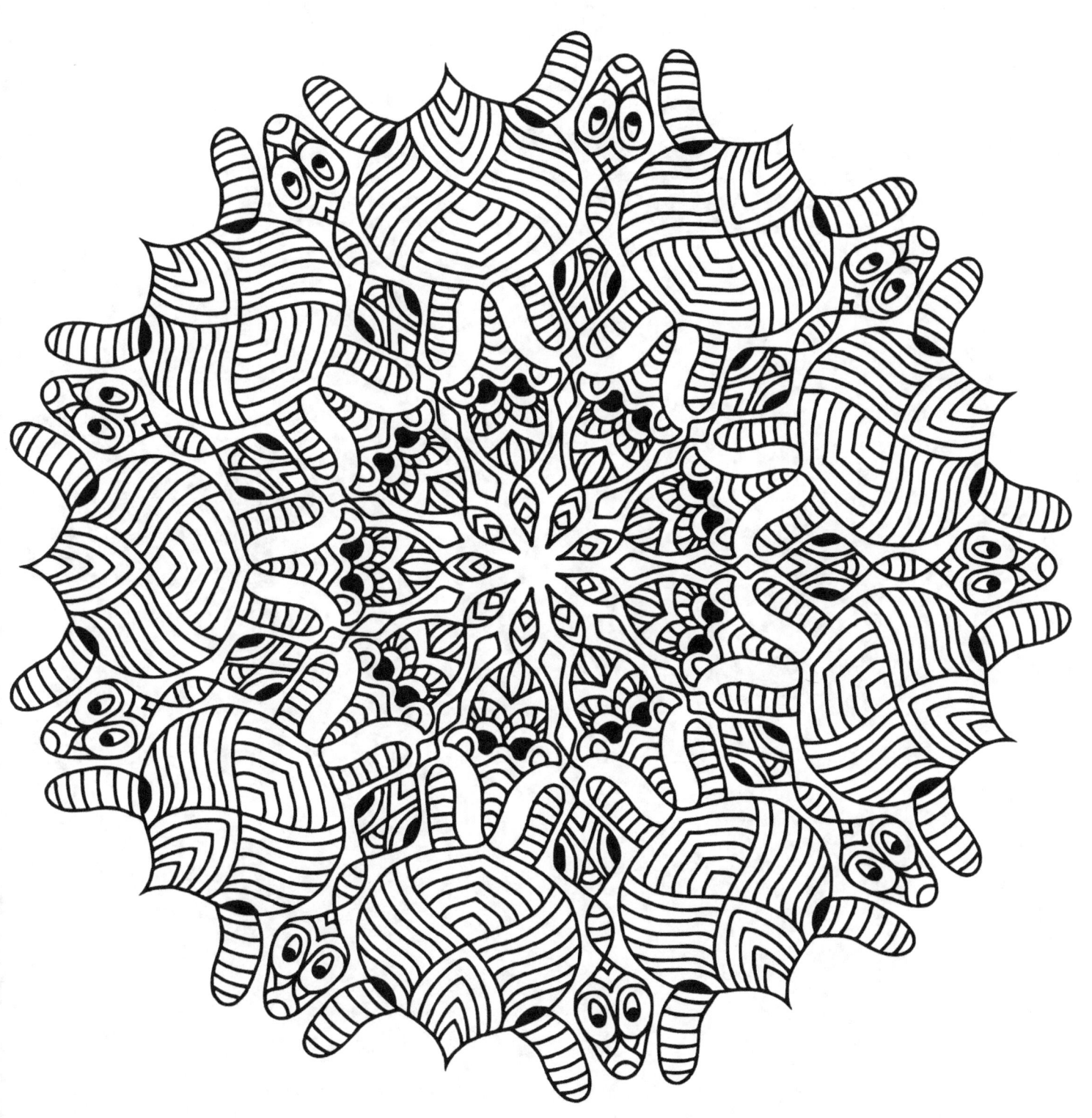

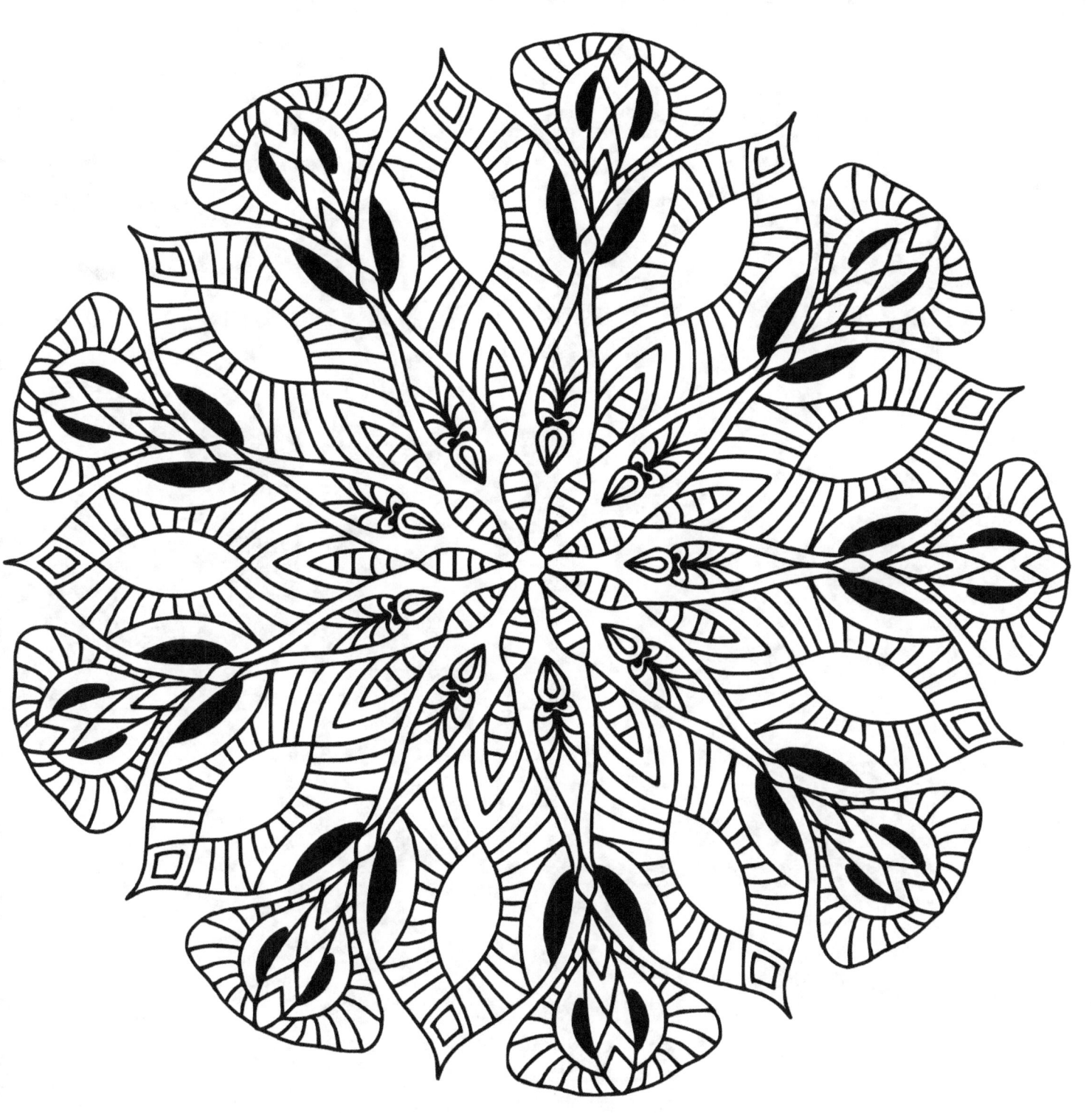

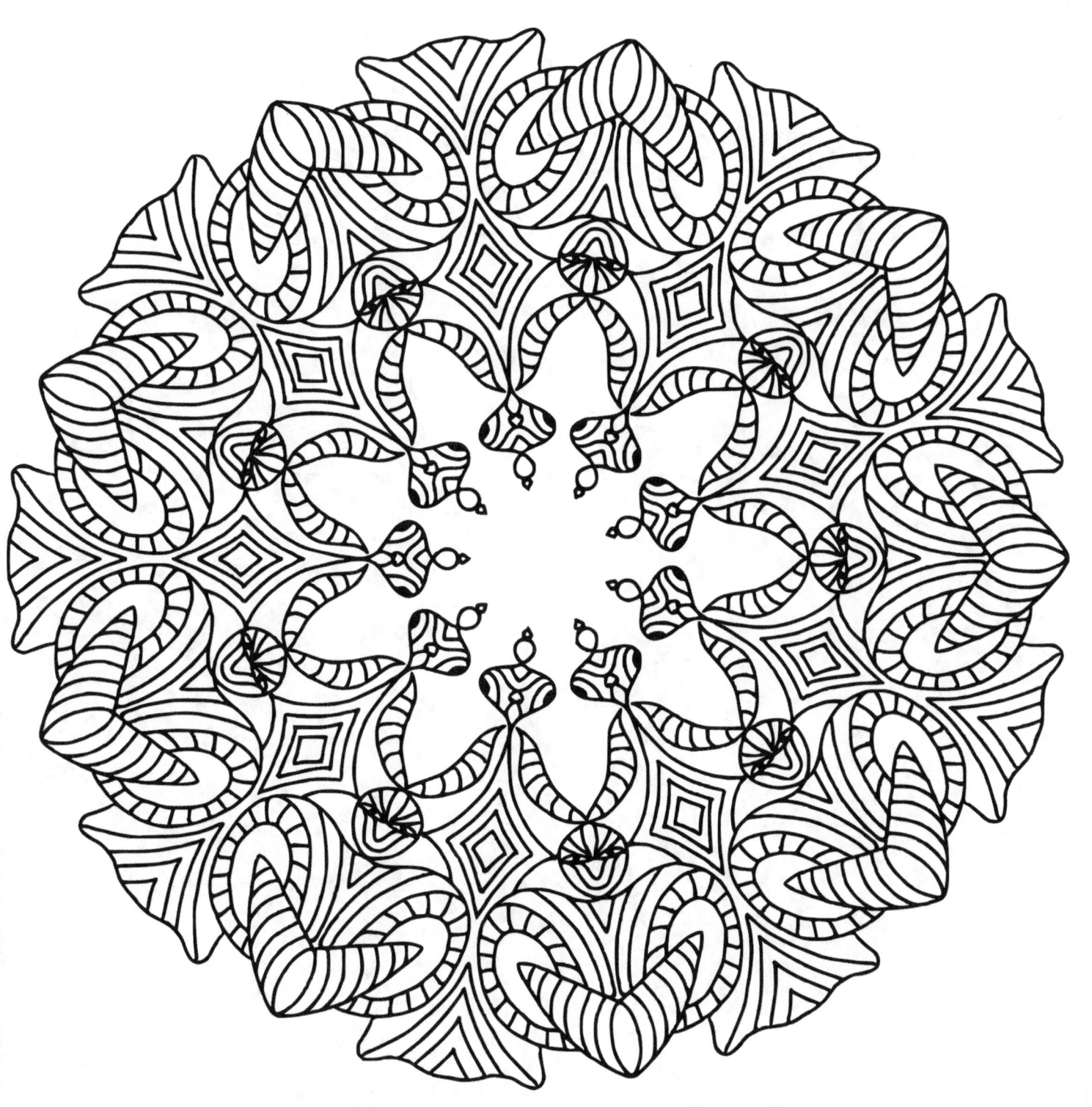

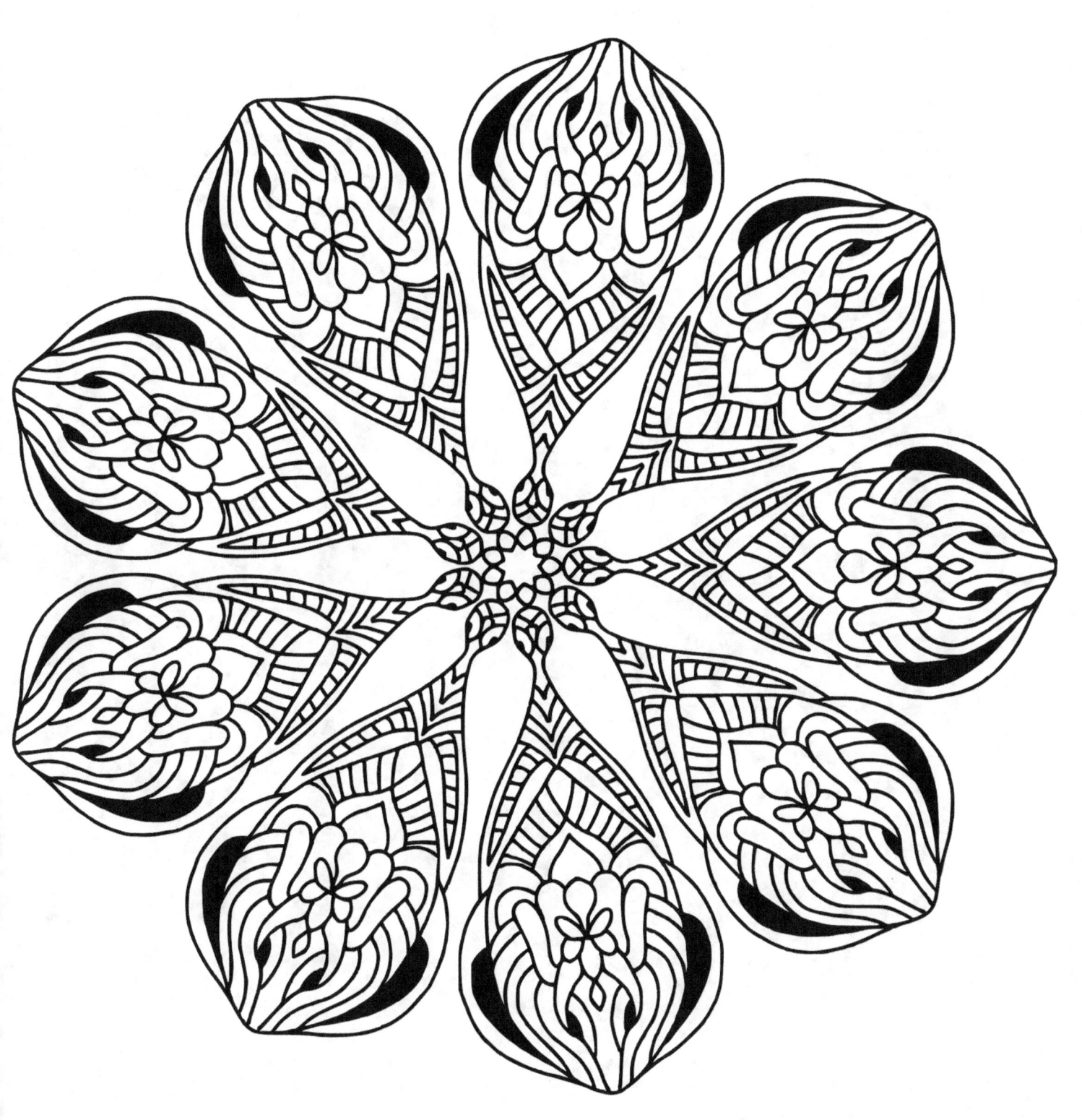

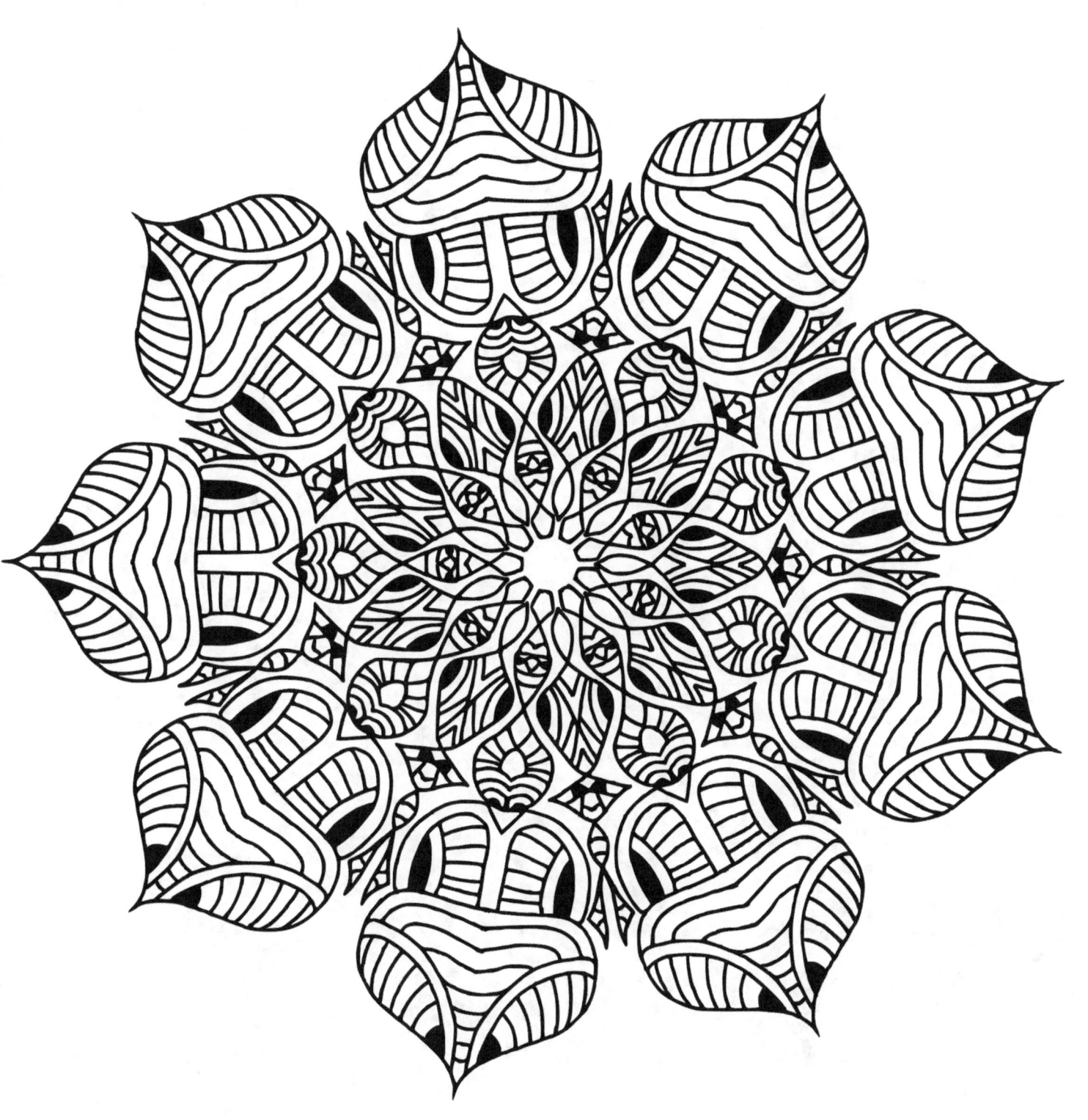

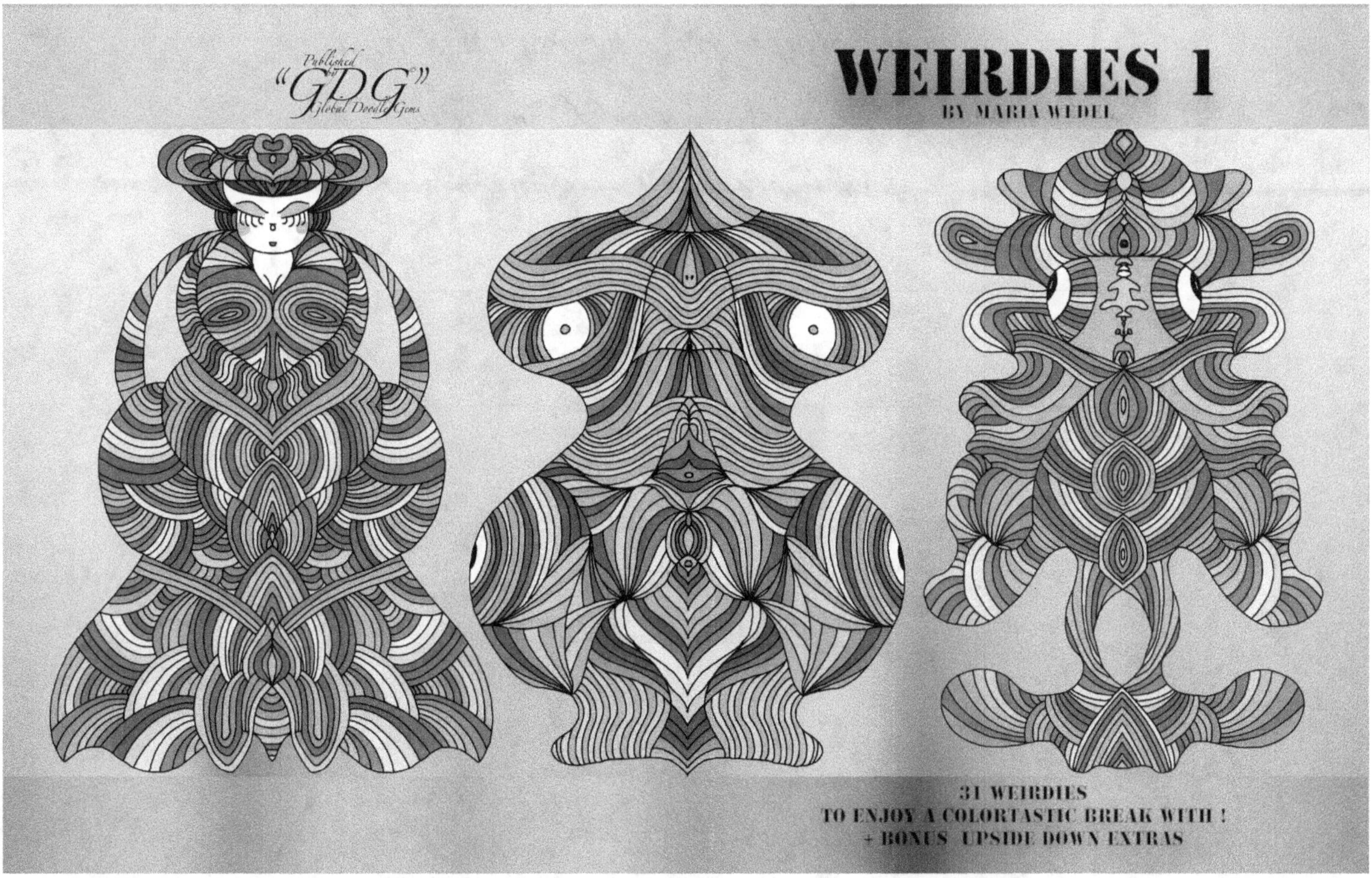

WEIRDIES 1
BY MARIA WEDEL

Published by "GDG" Global Doodle Gems

**31 WEIRDIES
TO ENJOY A COLORTASTIC BREAK WITH !
+ BONUS UPSIDE DOWN EXTRAS**

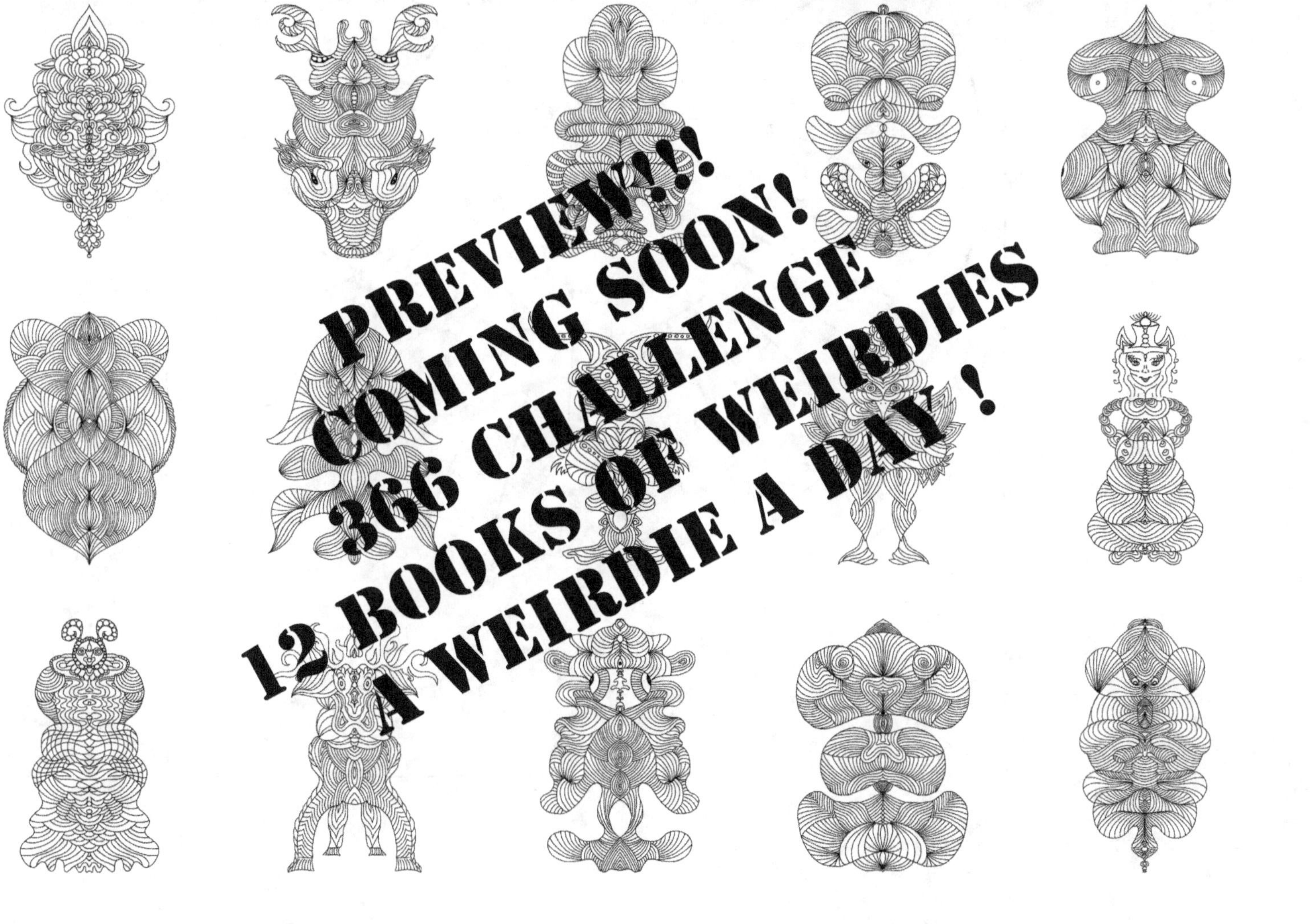

**PREVIEW!!!
COMING SOON!
366 CHALLENGE
12 BOOKS OF WEIRDIES
A WEIRDIE A DAY !**

Test your colors here on the samples from
"My Pocket Coloring Companion"
&
"My Coloring Companion"

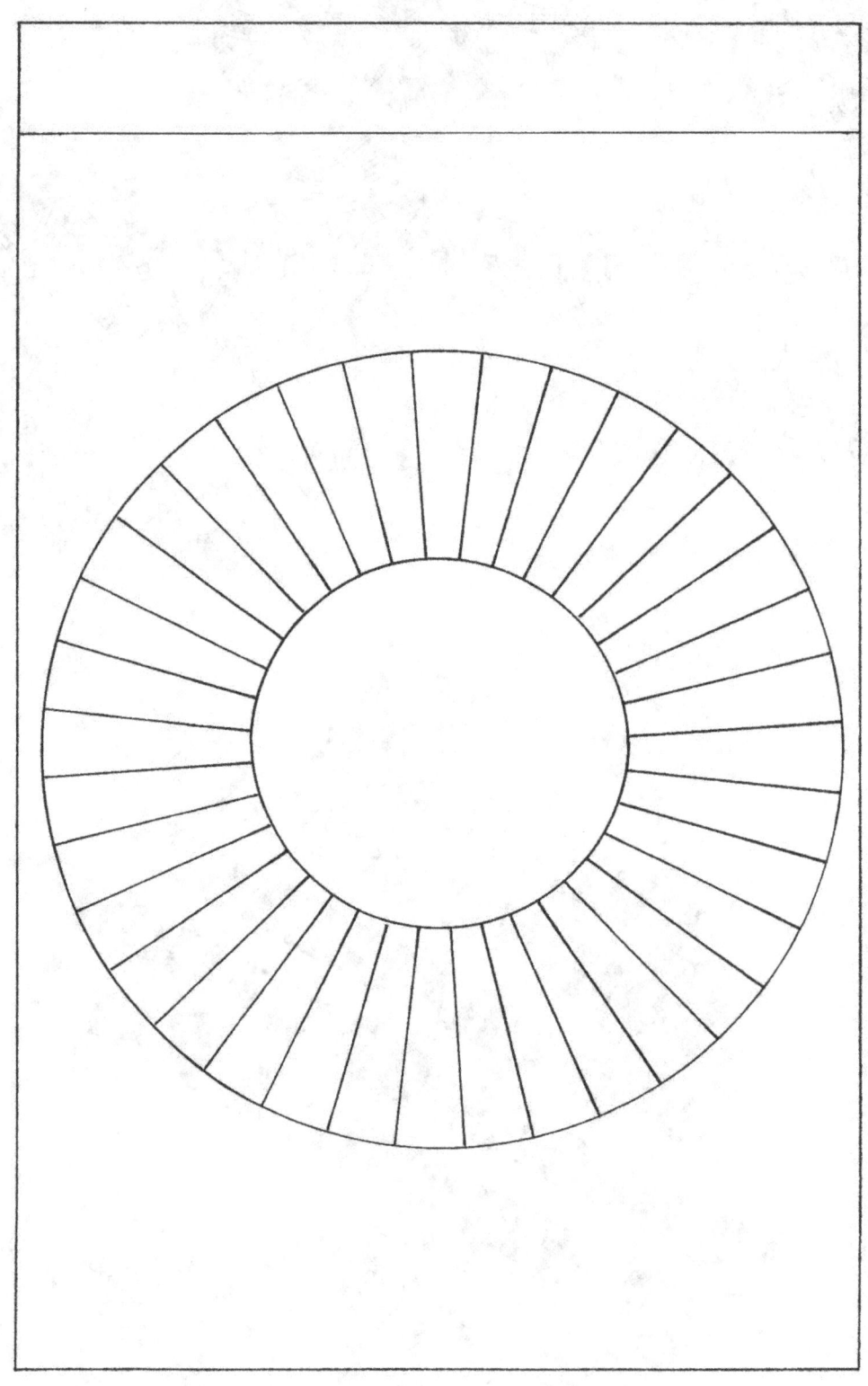

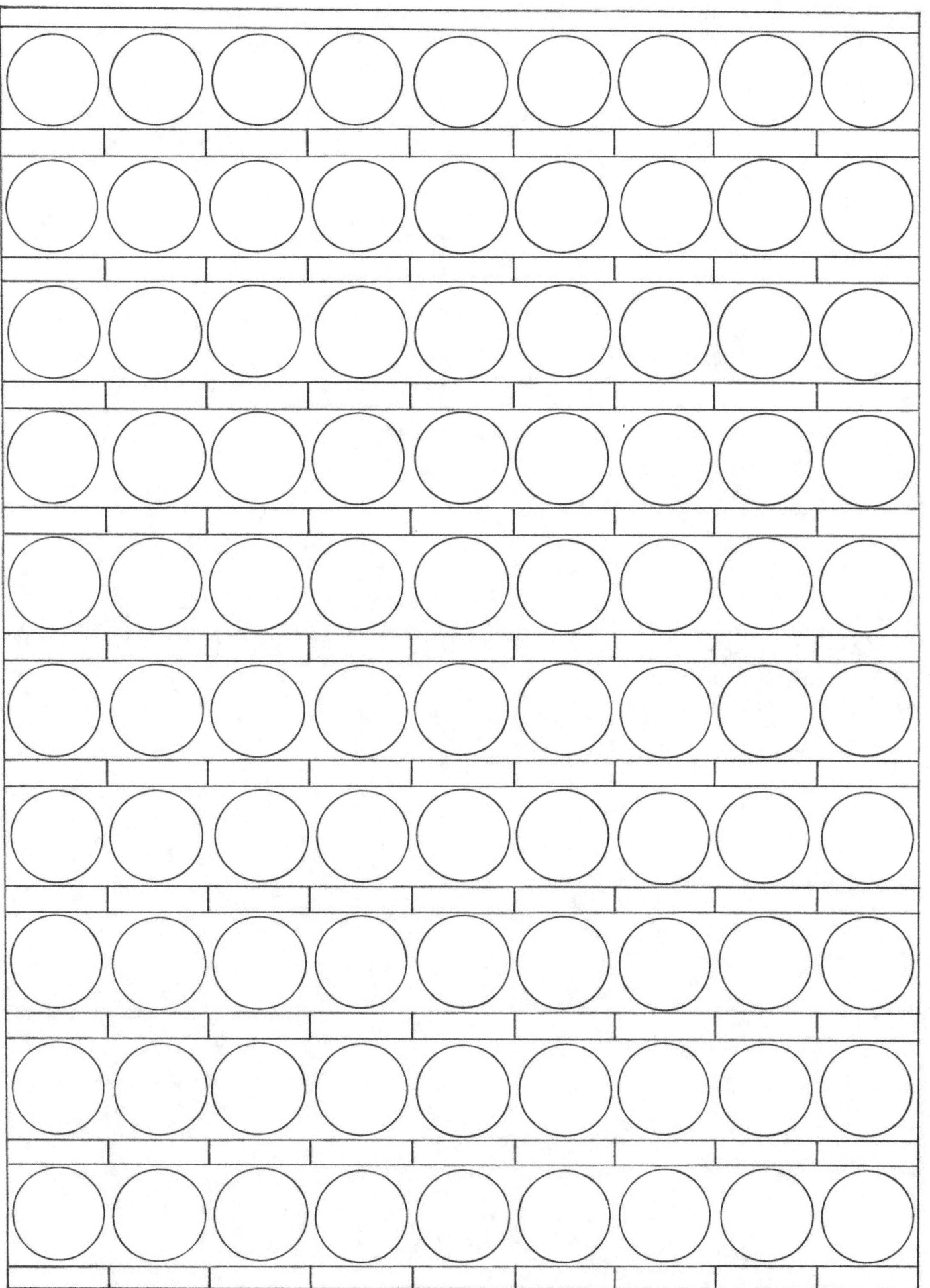

www.ingramcontent.com/pod-product-compliance
Lightning Source LLC
Chambersburg PA
CBHW082341220526
45470CB00008B/2596